CODE 4

LIFE ON THE STREET WITH A VETERAN COP

TERRY SMITH

TO GLORIA BLEEI

APRIL, 2023

CONTENTS

Contact: terrysmithauthor.com/contact

Published in the United States by Gunmetal Press, LLC.

Library of Congress Control Number: 2021914208

Code 4: Terry Smith

Although the author and publisher have made every effort to ensure the accuracy of information contained in this book, we assume no responsibility for errors, inaccuracies, omissions, or inconsistency thereof. Any slights of people, places, or organizations are unintentional. Dialogue is reconstructed.

ISBN 978-1-7368523-0-9 (paperback)

ISBN 978-1-7368523-1-6 (e-book)

Printed in the United States of America

BIO027000 Biography & Autobiography/Law Enforcement

Photographs are property of the author unless otherwise noted.

10 9 8 7 6 5 4 3 2 1 First Edition

In memory of my oldest grandson, Jesse, who left us too soon.

FOREWORD

Terry Smith was the first BCA senior agent who would work with me. When I joined the BCA's Organized Crime Intelligence Unit, I was just out of college *and* female, the first woman agent hired at the Bureau of Criminal Apprehension (BCA). Most BCA agents had been hired from other police agencies with prior investigative experience. I was hired along with two other male agents right out of college, with no police experience. We brought the average age of an agent down considerably.

I would like to think that it was my lack of experience which caused the hesitancy, but in reality, women officers were rare in police work at that time. Those who were working in other agencies typically worked juvenile or sexual assault investigations and were not considered "real cops." They would have never been considered for general investigative or patrol assignments. There was skepticism as to a female's capability for physical strength, judgment in a crisis situation, or whether we could "back-up" a male officer.

As years progressed, it was recognized that women brought different skills to the job and could be equally successful. Terry became my mentor, teaching me the steps to build a solid case, to conduct surveillance, to write a search warrant, the how-to's of undercover work and the many intricacies of investigative work. He challenged me to be the best investigator that I could be and never treated me as less than equal.

As years went by and we took separate paths in law enforcement, Terry's career brought him to Bemidji, Minnesota, to command a team of BCA investigators, and my career diverged into university and then municipal policing as a Chief of Police. Terry continued to remain a sounding board, a consummate teacher and a state leader in complex case investigations. After recognizing the need to train local law enforcement in how to appropriately handle death scenes and when to call for state investigative services, Terry provided statewide training for officers on how to conduct death investigations and produced a wallet card with basic questions to ask upon arriving at a death scene. My departments benefited from his training.

As a police officer and law enforcement executive, he was tough, yet compassionate; strategic, yet humble; serious, yet with a wicked sense of humor; and he always followed a moral compass in his work. The memories that Terry Smith has written about in this book are just a few of the ways that he has touched the lives of so many: families of victims, perpetrators, police officers, law enforcement support personnel, prosecutors, defense attorneys and judges as well as the community at large. I am truly blessed to call him my mentor and friend.

Joy M. Rikala
Minnetonka, Minnesota, Chief of Police (retired)

PREFACE

One evening in the fall of 1965, I walked into a gym at Portland Junior High in Bloomington, Minnesota. I was there for a screening program that would winnow through a crowd of applicants and select a handful of them to be Bloomington police officers. I almost turned and walked back out again when I saw that there were hundreds of other candidates. *Surely they'll never pick me out of this crowd*, I thought. Still, I stayed and went through a long evening of physical agility and written testing. At the end of the evening one of the leaders of the event read out a list of about 35 candidates who were to report for further testing on the following Saturday. Astonishingly, my name was one of them.

The next two Saturdays were long, hard days of further testing and interviews. Our numbers dwindled but I was still in the mix. The process went on for several more weeks and culminated with a final meeting with the chief of police. At the end of this conversation, the chief said, "I don't usually hire people as young as you (22) but I'm going to take a chance on you." In January 1966, I stood with seven other young men to be sworn in. Bloomington was a well-run, top-notch department. It was a great place to learn how to be a cop. I thrived on the feeling of being on the edge, not knowing what was coming next. I loved doing something that made differences for good in the lives of people who needed my help. In my time on that job, I hope I gave as much to them as they gave to me.

In 1973, I went to work for the Organized Crime Intelligence Unit (OCIU), a small organization working under the Minnesota Attorney General. Two years later, the OCIU was absorbed by the Minnesota Bureau of Criminal Apprehension (BCA), best described as the detective division of the state police. I worked out of the BCA's St. Paul Office until 1986 when I was promoted to Special Agent in Charge of the Bemidji Regional Office, headquarters for operations in the top half of the state. I retired in 2003.

From the first day I donned a police uniform until the day I retired, I was privileged to do what I felt I was born to do. It was a life of action and adventure, danger and trauma, excitement and fleeting bursts of fear. Most remarkable were the people who accompanied me on this journey—men and women who didn't shrink away from peril, who were comfortingly calm in the midst of pandemonium, who could be hard-edged or kind as circumstances demanded. Day and night they kept watch so that the rest of the world could go on about its business untroubled. My story is also theirs.

The words that follow are anecdotes and observations from my experiences along the way. Had I been in some less action-filled profession, any one of the accounts I give here could have been a highlight of my life. A 37-year span of such stories makes them all run together until something triggers a memory of a specific situation. Sometimes when I think back over my working life, I wonder, *Did those things really happen?*

Most of my stories are told from a male perspective. In my era, women had not yet come on board in significant numbers. In the old Bloomington days, Pat Downey, who was assigned to the Juvenile Bureau, was our only female officer. There were none who worked in uniform. Later, at the BCA, women had begun to enter the ranks, but not to the extent that they exist now.

I can't imagine having done anything else or anything better with my life. Of course, it helps that I survived it all, never took a bullet, was never badly hurt, never had to shoot anybody. Any of those things can change one's entire experience. Several fellow officers paid with their lives for stepping into harm's way. Others experienced a slower death, sinking into alcoholism when an aspect of the job became too much for them. I think of them from time to time and feel some sorrow for the meaning that "Protect and Serve" held for them.

I came away from all of this with a great love for the police profession. I won't say I love all cops because there are some that don't deserve that level of regard. It's a group of mostly good people, though, in a noble occupation that seems to be getting more difficult as the days go by. And so, I dedicate this writing to all who still put on a Kevlar vest each day and head out to see what triumphs or tragedies may come their way.

Terry Smith

1

TOUGH GUYS

Cops are tough. Everyone expects that. If you wake up in the middle of the night to the sound of someone breaking into your house, you don't call 911 and say, "Send me a wimp!" Your ideal first responder is someone who bench presses five-hundred pounds, can shoot the ears off a gnat, and has a surly attitude toward middle-of-the-night burglars. Many cops don't fit that profile exactly, but everyone who pins on a badge knows that sometimes non-deadly force is the only way to take someone into custody or to get a situation under control. When that time comes, you can't run away and you can't afford not to win. A lost fight could mean a lost life, a realization that hovers over every confrontation.

People assume that carrying a gun gives the police an advantage in every fight. That's often not true. The use of deadly force is carefully limited by law, and an officer knows that shooting when he shouldn't, could make him the defendant in a homicide trial.

I'm six feet tall and 180 pounds, not an imposing figure. I'm sure that most of the people I dealt with were not impressed by my physical presence but were influenced by society's general respect for a uniform, badge, and gun. Some rightly presumed that, even if they could take me, they wouldn't have a chance against the reinforcements that would show up if I called for help. I always tried to treat everyone respectfully, in part because I like people, but also because I wasn't going out of my way to get into struggles. In spite of all of this, there were quite a few occasions when I had to fight someone into the handcuffs or pull him away from someone else. Some of these situations turned into real brawls. I'm still bemused to be able to report that I never lost one of these.

One of the scariest fights of my career came when I had only been on the department for a few months. I was working a day baseball game at old Metropolitan Stadium where the Twins played during the Harmon Killebrew era. There were about twenty of us working each game. We'd get a traffic direction assignment for a few hours before the start, then go into the stadium to an assigned area where we'd watch a little baseball and deal with any problems the ushers brought to our attention.

I was walking down the stadium's main hallway when a man deliberately stepped into my path, put his hands on his hips, and said, "I can whip any ten cops here." My first reaction was, *He's under-estimating.* He was huge and rugged looking. Although around my age, he was about six inches and a hundred pounds bigger than I. His beer-breath told me that alcohol had helped bring us to this moment of confrontation.

I was willing to ignore his challenge. It could have ended there. If he had a friend who could take charge of him and get him sobered up, he'd probably just feel sheepish later about his behavior at the ball game. Any such possibility was gone when he reached out and gave me a shove. He'd crossed the line and the fight was on.

I like to read and have enjoyed a number of Louie L'Amour's Western novels. In nearly every one of his books, there's at least one fight scene that goes on for two or three pages with vivid descriptions of every punch, kick, gouge, and body slam. In real life, it's not that way; the average fight probably lasts fifteen or twenty seconds, and when it's over, no one has a clear recollection of exactly what happened. In this situation, I can only tell you that the man lunged at me, I somehow side-stepped and misdirected him and took him down hard on the concrete. As he hit the deck, every one of my 180 pounds slammed down on top of him. He was stunned by the force and it gave me a moment to twist his right arm up behind his back and get it handcuffed. At that moment Orv Harrison, another officer, came along and helped me get the other wrist cuffed. The other cops were amazed to see me leading this immense but subdued prisoner into the first aid room where we held him until the area squad came and picked him up. I was pretty surprised myself.

Met Stadium was the scene of one other memorable fight. I was working field security on the sidelines of a Vikings football game when a fan jumped the railing and ran onto the field. The cops don't run after people who do that unless they pose a significant threat to someone on the field. Instead, the ushers and civilian field security get the honor of chasing them down and escorting them to the sidelines where they are delivered into police custody for a misdemeanor violation.

In this case, the young misdemeanant had obviously done it as a lark and was smiling as I took his arm and led him off the field into the tunnel. Once out of the public eye, I would have frisked and cuffed him. Unfortunately, and much to my irritation, one of the ushers who had chased him down kept jawing at him as we left the field, berating him for his stupidity. I could see the situation going downhill as the railing-jumper became more and more angry and began shouting back at the usher. Suddenly, the man tore away from my grasp, grabbed the usher and slammed him into the tunnel wall.

At this point, even though there were several other people in the tunnel with us, the problem became all mine. In any struggle with a suspect, my instinct was always to try to take the opponent down forcefully and land on top of him. I was fast enough to use the momentary shock of a hard landing to twist an arm behind a back with enough leverage to subdue even the big strong ones. In this case, as the suspect was body slamming the usher, I was going for a head lock, then throwing him over my hip to that wonderful concrete stadium floor. Even though he was quite a big man, the cement took about seventy-five percent of the fight out of him. After a bit more grappling, he ended up wearing the handcuffs. I'd just as soon have put them on the usher.

Domestic calls often got us into situations where some kind of force was necessary. In these family arguments, feelings ran very high. When we got there, they were already angry at each other, and at least one of them was now highly irked that we were on scene. Throw in some alcohol consumption—one of the common elements at these events—and it could be dangerous and explosive. Our department always sent two squads to a domestic so that we could attempt to deal with the combatants separately, and if people wanted to fight, one officer wouldn't have to handle it alone. Over time, I developed a short list of cops that I didn't like to go on domestic calls with. A few of them were deficient in diplomatic skills, and one or two just liked to fight and didn't seem to work very hard at defusing the situation. And, of course, once somebody took a swing at my partner, it became my fight as well.

Sometimes we went on calls to break up fights and simply pulled people apart. The local VFW was frequently used for wedding dances, and every month or two things would boil over there. Sometimes there were groups of people, some wearing tuxedos, throwing punches or chairs at each other. On one occasion the bridesmaids really got into it. I never liked fighting with women under any circumstances, but there's special risk involved in struggling with one in a strapless gown.

At another one of these joyous wedding celebrations, the groom was trading punches with one of his groomsmen. No one wants to hassle someone at his own wedding reception, so we pulled them apart and warned them to behave. As soon as I let go of the groom, he lunged at the other man again. After one more try, with the same results, we'd had enough and took the groom to jail. At about five o'clock in the morning, I happened to be at the police station when the bride came in, still wearing her wedding dress, to bail him out. I wonder how that marriage worked out.

Generally, bystanders don't step forward to help an officer who's trying to subdue someone. About three o'clock one morning, I brought a prisoner to the old General Hospital Emergency Room in Minneapolis to have some cuts stitched up before I took him to jail. At the doctor's request, against my better judgment, I took the handcuffs off the man's wrists. A moment later he bolted from the room, ran through the waiting area and out onto the sidewalk along Portland Avenue. I followed, hot on his heels. I tackled him after a spirited fifty-yard dash, got an arm up behind his back, and arrived at a stalemate. Most cops would tell you that little wiry guys can be harder to handle than big, slower ones. I got his one wrist cuffed but was unable to wrestle his other arm behind his back. I began to force his cuffed arm higher, shouting, "Bring your other arm back or I'll break this one!"

He continued to struggle mightily and kept shrieking, "Break it off! Break it off! Break it off!" I realized that, although I could keep him pinned down, I couldn't move or let go in any way. To my great relief, a Minneapolis Officer came driving by, saw us on the ground, and leaped out to help me get the man cuffed. During the struggle a cab driver was parked five feet away, elbow out the window, looking on with interest but offering no help. As I got to my feet, I think the cabdriver saw a hard look in my eye because he started his car and sped away.

One time, two men did come to my aid, and I'll forever be grateful. I'd stopped a car with two rough looking men in it. Unexpectedly, both turned out to have arrest warrants. I told the passenger to stay in the car and took the driver out, telling him he was under arrest. The driver tried to break away from me and we began to struggle down on the pavement. As we fought, I was desperately trying to watch for the passenger, afraid that he'd jump on my back or try to grab my gun.

As I cuffed the driver, I heard the wonderful words, "We're with you officer!" A man and his teen-aged son had seen the struggle and ran to watch my back until I could get both suspects under control. I hope that, in my exhausted, agitated state, I gave them the thanks they deserved.

Several times I responded to calls to assist with a diabetic who was suffering an insulin reaction. This can have the odd side effect of making a perfectly nice person act like a mean drunk. The cure for this is to have the individual ingest something with sugar in it. They know it, their family knows it, but sometimes the chemical imbalance in their system throws them into an obstinate rage. Combative as these people could be, I would have felt terrible about subduing someone in that state. Instead, I reasoned, cajoled, persuaded—any alternative to fighting someone who only deserved my help and sympathy. In each case, we eventually got there without violence, but all of these incidents taxed my diplomatic skills.

Police officers today have some tools that we didn't have when I wore a uniform, and I'm sure they are trained better. Still, it's impossible for them to do their job without occasionally getting into physical struggles and sometimes fighting for their lives. Modern cops must do the same job we did with the new possibility that any struggle may be captured by someone's cell phone video and forwarded to a news outlet. Then those who would never offer help, who know nothing of the desperation of fighting a battle that they must not lose, will be their judges. At their leisure, they will review and critique a few moments of fear and pandemonium and tell each other how the cops should have behaved.

I'm not on the job any more. I couldn't be, shouldn't be. But I'm very thankful that there are still people willing to do what we did: Run toward danger when everyone else is running away, risk losing their lives without shrinking back, race to the aid of someone in trouble, step between innocent people and those who mean to harm them.

CLOSE CALL

"Eight-oh-two, eight-oh-three—see a lady at the phone booth, 96th and Lyndale, on a domestic."

This call was unusual. The complainant was at a phone booth instead of at a home. My hunch was that the caller had either fled the house (upping the likelihood of a dangerous situation) or the dispute had happened out in public.

Officer Bruce Jones, a young spit-polished ex-military guy, and I arrived at the phone booth almost simultaneously and met a distraught, bruised woman. Her husband had been drinking heavily that evening and they had argued. He had become very physically abusive to her, finally throwing her to the floor and kicking her in the ribs. She broke away from him, grabbed the car keys, and ran out the door, shouting "I'm going to get the cops!" As she fled, she heard him shout back, "I'll be ready for them!" She said that her three small children were in the house with her husband. She was afraid he might kill them.

Over the years, I've seen the police response to dangerous situations evolve. SWAT teams with a lot of protective gear and the means to persuade a threatening person to surrender are now wisely used. It can be time consuming, but it saves a life now and then, and I'm in favor of it. However, this was the late 1960s and we didn't expect any help. We were cops. This was our job. So, we went to the house to deal with an angry husband and to get the kids out of a bad place.

It was a summer evening and nearly dark by the time we arrived at the house. I suppose at least a half-hour had elapsed since the woman had run from the scene. The place was completely unlit and spookily quiet. No raving drunk, no crying kids, nothing. Jones was a new cop and I'd been on for a couple of years. As the senior guy (probably 24 or 25 years old), I led the way as we crept to the back of the house, quietly opened the unlocked screen door, scanned the silent kitchen, and tip-toed in. We had our flashlights out but didn't have them turned on. There was just enough daylight to see dimly and we didn't want to give our positions away.

As we moved slowly and quietly through the kitchen, into the dining room, through the living room, down the hall, I concentrated on what might lie ahead. It was tense, slow progress.

I peeked into the first bedroom, saw nothing, then carefully gave it a better look. While I searched, Jones watched down the hall. We moved to the doorway by the second bedroom and repeated the routine. Nothing.

I have no explanation for what happened next. Maybe the adrenaline had worn off. Maybe I was convinced that the house was empty. Without reason, I relaxed. Instead of covertly peeking into the third bedroom, I stepped fully into the doorway. A man lay prone on the bed, a shotgun leveled at my midsection.

I'm dead! flashed into my head as I leaped to cover on the other side of the doorway. *He didn't shoot!*

Jones was still a few steps down the hall. He'd seen me leap but didn't know why. Hand signals, miming a guy with a gun, brought him to full combat mode and we crouched on both sides of the doorway, guns ready. I was about to shout at the guy to throw the gun down when I heard something that caused me to freeze. Jones heard it too. The man was gently snoring.

We took a few breaths, then, on my signal, ran through the door and pounced on the man, tearing the gun out of his hands. It was a twelve-gauge shotgun with a shell in the chamber and the safety on "fire." At the range of five feet or so, in those pre-body armor days, it would have torn me in two. He later admitted that he had intended to kill the first cop who stepped into the doorway.

We found the kids hiding under a bed. They hadn't been physically hurt that evening. I doubted that they could ever be okay in the larger sense, growing up in a home where that kind of violence occurred.

When the whole situation was over, I got into my squad car and drove away with a sick feeling in my stomach.

That was close.

MACE

I sometimes feel jealous of young police officers when I see the way they're outfitted today. They wear an array of equipment and weapons for any occasion: Kevlar vest, chemical spray, mag-light, extendable baton, taser, cell phone and portable radio, all topped off with a state-of-the-art semi-auto handgun.

In 1966, when I first pinned on a badge, we were issued a .38 special revolver, a flashlight, a set of Peerless handcuffs, and a gun belt to hang them on. The handcuffs came in a leather snap-fastened pouch that mounted on the gun belt. I carried them that way until the first time I had to fight someone into the cuffs. I then found how difficult it was to keep a screaming, fighting person on the ground, hold his arm up behind his back, get the cuffs out, and orient them to snap onto his wrists. On my first day off after such an event, I went down to Weitzman's Police Supply in Minneapolis and bought a hand cuff loop that hung to the right of my belt buckle. It kept the cuffs loaded in just the correct position where I could grab them with my right hand when I needed them. Most of us picked up some kind of night stick. No one had a portable radio; once we got out of the car, we were on our own.

I had been on the department for a while when we were issued Mace, a brand-new product that was meant to give us a way to take the fight out of a hostile person without using the time-honored police technique of smacking him with something. It came in a hard plastic aerosol can that fit in its own little holster on the gun belt. Typical of that era, there was no real effort to train the users. It was assumed that we could figure out the importance of directing the spray nozzle at the crook and pushing the trigger mechanism with our thumbs. If we hadn't grasped the entire program right away, we'd have it down by the second time we used it.

There was a learning curve. One of the cops hosed down an unruly customer in a restaurant and found that the stuff not only worked on the bad guy but on a number of well-behaved customers as well. In fact, he pretty well shut the restaurant down for the night. We used it as a threat without actually pulling the trigger a few times. There was a ferociously strong, very surly fellow who would get drunk and beat up his wife fairly often. We had learned by experience that it took about four cops piling on him simultaneously to get the cuffs on. When Mace came out, we were pleasantly surprised to learn that he had heard all about it and was scared to death of being sprayed. From then on, two guys and a can of Mace were all it took. The department overtime bill was significantly reduced, not to mention lowered costs for night stick replacements and band aids.

We hadn't been outfitted with this new tool for long when Officer Keith Stone and I got into a battle royal with a prisoner. We'd actually gotten him into the booking room in the jail and had taken the cuffs off when he went crazy. It's hard to fight with someone in a confined space. It's hardly an advantage to outnumber the fighter because you have to take turns getting at him.

I have to confess that, once the fight started, it didn't even occur to me that I might be able to bring it to a quick end with a well-placed shot of liquid tear gas. Somewhere during the struggle, Stone must have remembered the new element in the force continuum because I noticed he had it in his hand. The problem was, the guy was putting up such a fight that Keith couldn't seem to get the canister properly aimed or find the trigger with his thumb. Finally, in desperation, he raised his right fist high and brought the bottom of the Mace can down with a tremendous smack on the suspect's forehead. The man dropped like a rock and lay groaning on the floor with a neat little half-moon bruise on his forehead.

Stone looked at the black cylinder in his hand and said, "Hey, this Mace works pretty good."

DOG WATCH

W hen I started in Bloomington, the uniformed cops worked four shifts, rotating on to the next shift every two weeks. After a couple of weeks working days, we went to mid-shift (4:00 P.M. to midnight). Fourteen days later, it was the power shift (8:00 P.M. to 4:00 A.M.). The final one in the rotation was "dog watch" (midnight to 8:00 A.M.). The net result of all of these changes was that my body's internal clock was always set for some other time zone.

Some guys dreaded the all-night assignment. I looked forward to it because, even though things could get pretty slow about four or five o'clock in the morning, the potential for something good (defined in the police lexicon as a felony pinch or a hair-raising call) was always present.

There was a predictable rhythm to the dog watch. It started out busy. As soon as we got into our squads, we were answering bar calls, domestics that hadn't quite reached the boiling point during the mid-shift, and the occasional medical emergency. Traffic was still fairly busy, but it was different from daytime traffic. There were more people who had been drinking or who were "up to something" than during other portions of the 24-hour cycle. In between calls, I drove the streets of my district, scrutinizing every car, stopping every one-tail-lighter, working the percentages. I had plenty of arrests that started out with a simple traffic stop for a small infraction.

A good cop knows the cues that lead him to look for other types of misbehavior. Unusual nervousness was an obvious one, but there were others. I always watched what people did as they were pulling over after I'd hit the red lights. Sometimes it was obvious that they were trying to cover something up or shove it under their seat. A driver who jumped out and started to come back toward the squad might be trying to keep me from seeing something in his car.

One night a pretty good pinch fell right into my lap. I looked at the driver's license that had been handed to me and was unsure how to say the unusual last name.

"How do you pronounce your last name, sir?" I asked. He replied with an entirely different name than that on the license. It turned out he was using several false identities and had forgotten who he was supposed to be when surprised by my question. When I figured out who he really was, I learned there were warrants out for his arrest.

After about 2:30 or 3:00 in the morning, there was a subtle shift in our behavior. The calls slowed way down and we started gravitating toward whatever our individual enforcement tendencies might be. A guy who liked to write tickets might go sit on a four-way stop sign and write up everyone who rolled the sign. We had a few notorious "lover hunters" who spent their time sneaking up on steamed-up cars parked in out-of-the-way places.

My goal at that time of night was to make a felony pinch. One of my early mentors on the department, Roger Pedersen, taught me to go into a hyper-sensitive stealth mode, scanning every parking lot, looking between buildings, scrutinizing every sign of movement. I cruised lights-off behind businesses and warehouses, looking for a broken window or a door ajar. I knew every pry mark on every door and could spot a new one at a glance. I sneaked up on car lots and stood on top of my squad, scanning for people taking advantage of what we called "midnight auto supply." I imagine the guy who relieved me on the day shift wondered why there were footprints on the fenders and top of the squad. Even in the winter, I drove with my window open in order to hear breaking glass or a scream. Over time, this helped me arrest several burglars, various kinds of thieves, and a man raping a woman in a car in the parking lot by Eddie Webster's Bar.

One night while cruising through the parking lot by Essex Square Apartments, I came upon a young woman struggling to get away from a man who held her from behind in a bear hug. I jumped out, thinking I was about to arrest a sexual predator, and was surprised when it seemed he was glad to see me. It turned out they had been boyfriend and girlfriend until that evening when he had told her he wanted to date other women. She'd attacked him and the only way he could defend himself was to hang on to her. She'd also grabbed his wallet, shoved it down inside her pantyhose, and refused to give it back. It took quite a while to convince her to give up the wallet and let him leave peacefully.

Sometimes a night went from quiet serenity to fast action mode in a moment, finding a pried open door on a business or seeing someone run from behind a building. One of the most startling things that ever happened to me in the middle of the night occurred one morning about 3:00. I'd just cleared from a call at a house and walked to my squad which was parked on the street. It was a beautiful starlit night and I stopped for a moment to look at the sky. As I turned to reach for the car door handle, I looked down to find a huge rat standing about two feet away from me. When I came back to earth, we squared off to do battle. The rat finally went down for the count. By that time, though, my hickory night stick was in pieces.

There was a time, somewhere around 4:30 or 5:00 in the morning, when it was difficult to stay awake. That was a good time to pull up window to window with another squad and shoot the breeze for a few minutes. It was also a perfect time to drive down one of the deserted streets and see how many streetlights in a row I could turn off by hitting their light sensors with my spotlight.

As the sun came up, it would start to get busy again. There were a few traffic accidents, occasionally an early morning medical emergency, or a call from a business owner reporting a break-in that we hadn't spotted during the night.

At ten minutes to eight, if we weren't held over by a call, we'd pull up to the curb at the PD where the day shift cops were looking well-rested and ready for anything. After putting in a long, tiring night, I knew why the guy waiting for me was called my relief.

5

COP CARS

I'll always remember my first experience of getting up in front of my class in school and doing a solo presentation. It was startling to become suddenly aware that everyone was looking at me. Whatever I did, good or bad, clever or stupid, would be played out for an attentive audience. It was far more attention than I was used to receiving and it was unnerving. A few years later, I experienced roughly the same feeling when I got behind the wheel of a marked squad car and embarked on my maiden voyage in a black and white.

Everyone notices a police car as it approaches and most people react to it in some way: they check their speed, stop completely at stop signs, and become excessively polite to other drivers. They view the occupant of the squad car through a set of attitudes and experiences, sometimes favorably, sometimes unfavorably, sometimes with simple curiosity. Whatever the case, the person in the squad is always on display.

I started my career in the era when police cars were full-sized sedans with big V8 engines and rear wheel drive. The ones I first drove were '65 Fords. Fresh from the factory, I'm sure they were pretty high-powered machines. The problem was they were driven 24 hours-a-day in city traffic, 100 miles or more per 8-hour shift. These were the days of carburetors and points and plugs that needed changing every 10,000 miles. As the miles piled up, each car developed its own list of ailments and performance could be pretty questionable. One night Pete Govednik, a young cop who had started the year before me, made a traffic stop at 89th and Portland. As he got up to the car, several men leaped out and attacked him. He was just able to break away and get back to his squad where he shouted into his microphone his location and that he needed help. Everyone responds to a situation like that. I was a few miles away and screamed down onto 494 to get across town to Portland Avenue. Floored, on the freeway, my bucking, sputtering car topped out at 65 mph. Fortunately, other guys got there more quickly, and Govednik's assailants were all handcuffed and rethinking behavioral choices when I arrived.

Now days, a police officer wouldn't know how to use some of the equipment in those old squads. They had mechanical sirens on the right front fenders, big cylindrical turbines with slots all around the outside. The faster the turbine spun, the higher and louder the sound of the air being pushed through the slots. The siren was activated by stepping on a switch just above the driver's left foot. Hold the switch down, and the siren would wind up to its highest tone. Let up, and it would come back down again. The first time I did an emergency run at night, I found that when I activated the siren, it drew so much current that the headlights would go out. I learned to hit the siren, let up so the headlights would come back on, take a look at where I was going, and hit the siren again. The turbine inside the siren had tremendous momentum and would keep turning for a long time after you were done with it. There was a siren brake button that you pressed and held in to stop it. At any given time, the siren brakes in several squads didn't work. If I was using one of those cars, I could go on an emergency call, take care of the situation, and come back to find my siren still quietly going "r-r-r-r-r-r-r-r-r." According to department legend, a couple of cops were trying to stop some felons in a car one night when the guy on the passenger's side decided to shoot at the fleeing vehicle. He rolled down his window, stuck his gun outside, and put a bullet through the siren. This was before my time. We were pretty glad when we got electronic sirens.

One of the first things I learned about emergency runs is that using a siren does not automatically clear a path for you. It sounds pretty loud inside the car and gives you the sensation that the whole world knows you're coming, but there are some remarkably inattentive drivers and others whose brains seem to lock up when something unusual happens. There's no way to predict what panicky moves they'll make when they suddenly become aware of what's happening. Once I was running with red lights and siren on the freeway. As I took the France Avenue exit ramp, there were several cars ahead of me at the stop sign. Rather than pull out of the way, the drivers at the head of the line in both lanes just sat there looking terrified and effectively blocking the street. I had to get out of my squad, run up to the front car, and tell him to pull around the corner and out of the way before I could continue on.

Those old squad cars had drum brakes rather than the disk brakes that are now universal. They worked fine under normal circumstances but tended to fade when they got hot. In a car chase, we'd focus on the suspect but also on other traffic. This meant as we came to an intersection, we'd brake hard, check for traffic, then floor it again to catch up. All of this high-speed braking heated the brakes up to where they became ineffective. Take whatever danger the situation itself carried, add a large dose of adrenaline, then throw in the realization that no matter how hard we stepped on the brakes the car wasn't slowing down, and we'd have a lot on our minds. Sometimes those situations ended with our car running into the one we were chasing because the squad car had become like a runaway horse and we couldn't rein it in.

Another serious deficiency of those cars: They didn't have air conditioning. On a steamy summer day, the best I could do was to drive with the windows down. After fifteen minutes I'd have a huge, embarrassing sweat ring under each arm and another in the middle of my back.

At the beginning of a shift, I would take over the car from the guy going off duty. One thing I always did was to take the shotgun from its mount on the dashboard and verify that the magazine was properly loaded and there was no round in the chamber. I never knew what someone else may have done or forgotten to do with the weapon. The shotgun was held in a lock that needed to be opened with a key. I always kept it unlocked when I was in the car, thinking that if I needed it, finding the key and opening the lock could be more than I would have time to do. More than once, I came into a situation in which I had to grab the gun and bail out.

Smokers had the upper hand in those days, so every squad car smelled like stale cigarettes. One of the guys liked to smoke cigars; if I got into the car after he'd been using it, I'd drive with the windows down for a while.

Pulling away from the curb, the black and white car I drove was so much more than just a means of transportation. It was my office in which I completed the paperwork that went with every call. It served as a temporary jail for those I'd taken into custody. It was a trauma center for victims who'd suffered physical or emotional injury. It was a place of refuge for terrified people, like the young woman I found huddled in a phone booth in the middle of the night. She had been assaulted by five men who gang raped her, debated whether to kill her, and threw her from their car in an unfamiliar area. As I drove with her to the police station, she lay sobbing across the passenger's seat. At the office, she was so afraid to have me leave her that she

wanted to walk with me when I went to another room to get a
report form.

As strange as it felt when I first drove a squad car, it didn't
take long for me to feel at ease. I knew that I was really acclimated one day when I realized that I was driving on an emergency run, siren wailing, red lights blazing, window open, elbow
in the breeze, thinking about what I was going to do when I got
off duty.

6

MINEFIELDS

I wasn't sure if I should write this chapter. My love of the police business and my high regard for most officers makes me reluctant to share anything that may cast a negative light on the profession. In the end, though, my instinct toward candor won out. I only hope, as you read this, that you will grant that one can pursue a noble calling and still have feet of clay.

I've never been much of a ladies' man. I met a girl when I was seventeen, fell madly in love with her almost right away, and persuaded her to marry me when I was just turning twenty-one. My bachelor days ended almost before they got started. So, it was a new and disorienting feeling to learn, as a young uniformed officer, that a lot of women are attracted to cops. My first discovery of this came one night when I was sent to a bar to deal with a rowdy customer. The trouble-maker, warned that the police were on the way, had left by the time I got there. I had a short conversation with the bartender, exchanged pleasantries with a few patrons, and took my leave. As I walked down the hallway toward the back door, I was surprised when an attractive young woman came up beside me, slipped her arm

through mine, and said, "You're so beautiful when you smile."
She suggested that she could be waiting there for me when I got
off duty. It was an astonishing offer and a completely new experience for me. Did I think about not going straight home to my
wife and my little son at the end of the shift? Not for a moment.
At the door I politely disengaged, got into the squad and drove
off. The trouble was, that wasn't the last time something like that
happened. Over time I learned that the easy availability of the
opposite sex was one of the minefields that a cop has to navigate
if he wants to survive in reasonable shape.

The police business is a people business. Every tour of duty
is a series of personal interactions, not of the organized formulaic
sort that a doctor, a lawyer, or an insurance salesman might have,
but quick-hitting ones, mostly with people who are not at their
best. Blood flows, tempers flare, fear seizes, and moments later
we're in the midst of it all, making it up as we go, solving problems, separating combatants, calming things down. The uniform,
the strong image, the fearless front that a cop projects seem to
stoke the fires of desire.

It's also a job with little direct supervision. As the shift
progresses, you move from call to call, some by yourself, some
with other officers. There are plenty of opportunities to have
private conversations (like the one I had at the bar) with anyone
you encounter. Put all of this together and it's easy to see how
one could get into trouble.

At first, I didn't think about any of this very much. I was
married to the only woman I'd ever loved, working at a job I
found exhilarating, and not looking for extramarital opportunities. Still, possibilities can come by surprise: a woman in a filmy
nightgown who wants you to walk through the house with her to
make sure the prowler she thought she heard isn't hiding there; a
girl who suddenly views you as her protector after you subdued
her violent boyfriend; a flirtatious waitress; a lady who's had a
few drinks and looks at you like some kind of trophy. Depending

on your mind set, you can view this as a whole new world of possibilities or as an area where you'd better take yourself in hand and be on guard. Over the years, I worked with a number of men who chose the first approach. It didn't work out well for most of them.

Most of the cops I knew fit into one of three categories: Many were good family men, didn't play around, maintained happy marriages, and, as far as I knew, had no guilty secrets. Some pursued what seemed to me a dangerous game of being married to one woman while keeping an eye out for opportunities with others. A few ignored all of society's rules, took romance wherever they could find it, and lived what looked like pretty unsatisfying and chaotic lives. One of the guys I used to work with was on his fourth marriage the last time I talked with him. I jokingly told him every time he finds a new love he might as well buy her a house and give her half of his paycheck since that's the way it will probably end up anyway.

Over time some guys moved from one category to another. I had just come on duty one night, working the easternmost district. As I drove by the Thunderbird Motel, I noted a squad pulled up under the canopy by the front door. *What's this?* I thought. *I haven't been out of the car yet. How could I have missed a call in my area?* I cruised up beside the other unit. There at the front desk, I saw one of the central district guys, leaning on the counter, laughing and talking with the knockout front desk clerk. It only took me a moment to decide to slide right on out of there, but it worried me. He was a top-flight officer, a good family man with a beautiful wife. He had left his busy district and exited his squad without checking out. (We had no cell phones or portable radios, so checking out was a big deal.) The girl he was talking to was strikingly pretty and it wasn't difficult to see what had brought him there. A few years later he was divorced, had married a second woman, then divorced again. He was a good man, ethical and honest in his professional life, but he followed a wrong compass heading and didn't make it through the minefield.

The most flagrant womanizers I worked with were some of the narcotics agents. Drug cops tended to be the wild men of law enforcement—flamboyant, tough, and often hard drinking. Their world was made up of other narcs, dope dealers, and snitches. Their hours were irregular, mostly afternoons and evenings, giving them flexibility and not much accountability when it came to what time they showed up at home. The combination turned out to be way more freedom than some guys could handle. Sex was common and casual among many who used drugs. Hookers, exotic dancers, and addicts knew what was happening on the streets and were good sources of information but needed to be kept at arm's length.

I once worked with a female informant who told me about an unfolding murder plot. Some outlaw bikers were planning to kill an associate with whom they'd had a falling out. If we could overhear their planning, we could make a good conspiracy to commit murder case as well as prevent the killing. Remarkably, she said she was willing to wear a body transmitter and, ultimately, testify. Minnesota has a "One party consent" law that allows conversations to be recorded legally if one party to the conversation agrees, even though the others are unaware of the recording. We were poised to make our case.

On the day we were to meet, I stopped by the informant's house to get her wired up. The bug we were to use was in a harness much like a shoulder holster for a gun. The bug would hang under one armpit with elastic across the wearer's back and around the other arm to keep it in place. I showed her the outfit and put it on over my shirt so she could see how to wear it.

"They'll see that!" she scorned.

"No, you put it on under your clothing," I told her.

"Oh," she said, suddenly enlightened. With that she whipped off her shirt, which proved to be the only garment she was wearing north of her equator, and smirked at me. "Help me put it on."

"Figure it out for yourself," I said, tossing her the bug and retreating to the front porch. I wasn't afraid of falling for her charms but was suddenly wary of what I might be accused of after I'd been alone with her. We went on and made the case, but I didn't have any more unchaperoned meetings with her.

There's something else lying in wait in the police universe, ready to seduce the unwary: the job itself. I didn't grow up wanting to be a police officer; I just fell into the job through a series of coincidences. It wasn't long after I started, though, that I was telling myself, "I love this." In fact, I couldn't get enough of it. Police work is an occupation in which one can be as good as he wants to be. I was driven to achieve excellence, and this was a job that was wide open for that. Because it was so satisfying, I'm sure I thought about my work much more than I should have and, sometimes, put it ahead of the needs of my family. I know I wasn't alone in this. Whenever a group of cops and their wives got together socially, the guys spent their time talking shop, mostly recounting on-the-job stories. The wives either looked bored or tuned out and formed their own group to talk about something more interesting.

There's an almost addictive quality to the feeling of being on the hunt for a good pinch or experiencing the action at an event that will be the lead story in the 10:00 news. It's easy to like it too much and to pursue it to the neglect of other important parts of your life.

Finally, the job can have a great effect on the way its practitioners view life, the world around them, and other people. A good percentage of a uniformed cop's time is spent in places that his parents warned him to stay away from. I only remember going on a call to a church one time, a medical emergency. On the other hand, calls to the lowest dives in town, places where drunkenness, anger, and debauchery prevailed were commonplace. Whatever we may have been like before, most of us developed a pretty tough attitude as we settled in to this line of work. Daily exposure to people who are dishonest or predatory in their treatment of others, sociopaths who can do terrible things without remorse, or victims of every kind of abuse can skew one's perspective. It isn't that we lost our ability to laugh or to speak politely as we conducted business; lurking just below the surface, though, was a hard-edged feeling of being on guard, of being not at all surprised when people acted badly.

In 1966, when I started on the job, the expectation both inside and outside of the department was that you would simply roll with whatever happened. Did you just hold a dead child in your arms? Or pull a crushed body from a wrecked car? Or risk death in a violent confrontation? Get over it; that's your job. Nowadays there's a much clearer understanding of the emotional price that is involved when experiencing a steady diet of violence and tragedy. Critical incident debriefing sessions and mandatory visits to psychologists are in the aftermath of many of these incidents. Sometimes those things help; sometimes they don't.

How did I handle my thirty-seven year trek over this dangerous ground? The results were mixed. I made a decision early on that there would only be one woman for me and I acted accordingly. I couldn't possibly have known then how glad I would be now that I kept it that way. So far, so good.

As I've already hinted, the job captured a big part of my life, perhaps bigger than I should have allowed. I liked it too much and focused attention there that should have been given to my family. Even years into retirement, I still feel some guilt about that.

It's difficult to know what kind of person I'd be if I had been in a different line of work. Many of the things I saw are still with me today. During the last seventeen years with the BCA, I supervised a squad of homicide investigators. I was at many death scenes and, in my mind, revisit them from time to time. I'm sure that the job had an effect on the way I view people and their motives. I may not always be as sympathetic as I should be toward people who aren't doing well, having long ago observed that many people create their own misfortune. I'm pretty sure that some people are bad, not because of some sociological trick that life has played upon them, but simply because they choose to be bad.

In spite of some of the negatives, I can't think of anything else that could have suited me as well as the path I followed or imagine having done it with less dedication. In this one-way trip we take through life, it's a great blessing to find one's perfect niche. I wouldn't want to have missed it.

7

RESCUE

I entered the police business with only a general idea of what cops actually did.

- Write traffic tickets—check.
- Arrest law breakers—check.
- Respond to traffic accidents—check.

Beyond those activities I couldn't have written any kind of job description for a uniformed police officer. It was surprising during my first days with a senior officer to find out how often people called on us to help them with an array of things they weren't prepared to handle. One of the most common calls for help was generically referred to as a "Medical," an emergency situation in which someone was injured or in physical distress. The dispatcher gave us an address, a terse description of the problem, and his estimation of the level of emergency.

"Eight-oh-two, medical at the Holiday Station, 84th and Lyndale, man down on the pavement, possible heart, code three." We took it from there.

In 1966, when I started my career, there wasn't the kind of

quick availability of paramedics and first responders that most of us now expect. Our most reliable ambulance service came out of Savage, Minnesota, with about a fifteen- or twenty-minute response time. The ambulance crew specialized in driving fast and not much else. The closest emergency room was at Fairview Southdale Hospital, an eight- to ten-minute whistle run up France Avenue. To a person whose heart had stopped beating or with an injury that was spurting blood, we were the only game in town.

Every squad was equipped with a well-stocked first aid kit and a resuscitator or an ambu for breathing assistance. Every cop developed a reservoir of experience for dealing with heart attacks, injuries, unresponsive victims -- and death. All of these occurred, not in the controlled environment of an emergency room, but on a sidewalk or a loading dock, in a car or a living room, at a business, all over the city. Sometimes the victim was trapped in wreckage or under something that had collapsed. Then the problem became tactical as well as medical.

I recall one accident on Highway 494 in which a semi-trailer had tipped over onto a taxi, smashing its roof down to the level of the hood and trunk. When I arrived on scene, the first thing I heard was a continuous high-pitched scream from within the flattened car. It took about twenty minutes for the fire department to cut away enough of the car to reach the victim, who never stopped screaming until he could see daylight again. As it turned out, the cab driver was the only one in the vehicle. He wasn't even badly hurt but had experienced an awful case of claustrophobic terror.

It didn't take long to figure out that the things people needed most from us were a calm demeanor and decisive action. Those at the scene were usually panicked, fearful, and flustered. Many of the victims hardly knew what had happened to them or how serious their situation was.

We had a lot of first aid training in rookie school. I went

along on a number of medical calls while I was still a ride-along
neophyte. Still, it was daunting to take on the responsibility of
working alone, knowing that I had only experienced a sampling
of the kinds of emergencies that were, no doubt, coming my way.
Sure enough, about three in the morning of my first night on my
own, I got a call that a child had stopped breathing. I raced to the
scene and was met at the door by a distraught mother holding a
six-month-old who was—dead. The baby was cold with no pulse
or breath. He'd probably expired some time before the mother
found him that way. Knowing this, my instinct was to attempt to
revive him anyway. I began CPR and was soon joined by another
officer who assisted me for a time, then told me it was no use.
For the sake of the mother, and even for myself, I was glad I had
given it everything I had.

Over time, I saw just about every kind of injury or physical
dilemma that people commonly experience; lots of heart attacks
and strokes, broken limbs, gashes, bruises, severed body parts,
unconscious victims, people in agony. I organized a group of
bystanders to lift a car from a seventeen-year-old girl. I bandaged
her exposed brain as she writhed on the ground. I crawled into
the mangled remains of a car to try to save a woman who was
pinned and bleeding to death. I sat next to a weeping mother in
the back seat of a squad car, giving mouth-to-mouth resuscitation
to her tiny infant as my partner sped toward the hospital. I ran up
flights of stairs carrying a heavy resuscitator, feeling like I could
use a shot of oxygen myself.

Shift after shift, we responded to situations that, after a
while, all ran together. Had I been in another line of work, any
one of them would have haunted my thoughts for a long time.
Here are a few that still stand out in my mind:

> A small boy, about three years old, had somehow put a golf ball
> in his mouth. His mother couldn't get it out, and the ball was
> acting as a check valve, blocking his airway. I was able to get

my thumb and forefinger behind the ball and pull it out enough for him to breathe. I suppose because he was scared and tense, he was unable to open wide enough to spit the ball out. Slowly, slowly I forced the ball out between his teeth, making him open so wide that some of the skin on the inside of his mouth actually split. His mother told me, as I was leaving, that she had never been so glad to hear a siren.

A man mowing a steep embankment with a walk-behind power mower pulled it back onto his foot, hacking off the front of his shoe and all of his toes. I bandaged up shredded bits of shoe, a mangled foot, and a few other odds and ends in a sort of surprise package for the emergency room docs to unwrap.

A man working at a hydraulic press in a factory forgot to remove his hand from the press table as the unit came down, severing all four fingers and most of his palm. All were smashed beyond any hope of reattachment, so we just bandaged up what was left and sent him to the ER.

I was only about thirty seconds away from the John Deere Plant when I was given a call to respond to the office there for a possible heart attack. The victim, a middle-aged man, had no pulse and was not breathing when I arrived. He was sagging in a chair, held there by his co-workers, who had no idea what to do. I quickly put him on the floor, cleared his airway, and had one of his co-workers hold the resuscitator mask to the victim's face while I began doing chest compressions. Soon Officer Curt Workman arrived to assist and we continued to work on the man until the ambulance arrived. Although we didn't usually accompany the ambulance to the hospital, it seemed, in this case, that there was a chance to save the man if we stayed with our rescue efforts. I went right along into the ambulance, straddling the man with my back braced against the roof to keep from being thrown off in the turns, continuing rhythmic chest compressions. At the hospital, ER staff members came out to meet us, put the paddles to the man's chest, and shocked

his heart back into service. A month or so later, the man came
to the police station to say "Thanks."

I responded to a multi-car accident at 35W and 494. In one
of the cars, I found a young man slumped across the front seat.
Getting no response from him, I crawled into the car and found
that he was dead, although he had no visible injuries. Before
his body was taken from the scene, I took his driver's license
from his pocket so I could identify him for my report. It struck
me that he was twenty-three, the same age as I was at the time.
How quickly everything can change for us.

Each one of these events carries its freight of emotions: fear,
anxiety, empathy, distress. Add to these situations steady exposure to mankind at his worst, and you might well ask, "What
emotional stamp does this put on police officers?" The answer,
of course, is individual as well as general. Some of my peers
took to the police officer's drug: alcohol. Some became more
callous than was good for them. Most of us, though, did pretty
well. We learned, almost subconsciously, to step into a traumatic
situation, care intensely while it was ongoing, and then let it go
when we'd done our part.

I seldom learned what happened to the victim after my job
was completed. I showed whatever kindness I could to those still
at the scene and left, ready for whatever came next. I will say,
though, that some of these things transcend the years for me.
From time to time, I can still feel a touch of sadness or grief
when one of them comes to mind. I'm glad that I retained that
much of my humanity.

A few years ago, my wife and I were walking along the
boardwalk in Duluth. We came to a group of people standing
together, then noticed a man lying on the ground. No one seemed
to know what to do. I found that he had no heartbeat and was not
breathing, so I began chest compressions while asking
bystanders to direct paramedics to the scene. When the para-

medics arrived, they took over the CPR effort. I spoke some words of comfort to a man who said he was the victim's friend, then we continued our walk. I never found out whether the man lived or died.

Just like the old days, I thought.

8

OUTLAWS

I'd been on the PD for about four years when word came to our detective division that members of the Outlaws Motor-cycle Gang, a Hell's Angels-like group, had moved into an old farm along the Minnesota River. I'm not sure whether the detectives had inside informant information or were simply presuming, based on the gang's reputation, that something bad would be happening at the farm. Detective Sergeant Butch LaBerge asked if I would be willing to join him in some nocturnal surveillance. When I happily agreed, he arranged for me to be relieved from uniform duty a few nights per week and the game was afoot.

The farm was very remote, only accessible by driving on old Cedar Avenue to the bridge, now closed, that crossed the river, then following a dirt road west for a mile or so. There were truck farming operations along the river, but people—other than the Outlaws—had given up on living there because of periodic flooding. At night, it was the most out-of-the-way place in Bloomington -- silent, black as a coal mine, and several miles by road from any other living human beings.

On the first night of our surveillance, Butch and I drove part way in, hid our car in a grove of trees, and walked along the tree line to the field behind the farm. There were lights on in the farm house. We could see that there was an old barn behind the house and a machine shed off to one side. We approached cautiously, keeping the machine shed between us and the house. At the shed, we crawled through a window, then climbed up into a loft where we could open a door slightly and look down into the back yard of the house from about one hundred feet away. As we watched during the next hour or two, we could tell that there were at least five or six people present in the house or, occasionally, out in the yard. Late that evening, as we were thinking of a stealthy with-drawal, we saw headlights coming down the road in our direc-tion. We watched a U-Haul van pull into the yard and a number of people spill out of the house. It was really too dark to see everything that happened, but it appeared that a motorcycle was unloaded from the van and wheeled into the barn. We were mighty glad that they hadn't brought it to the machine shed instead. When things settled down, we crawled back out through the window, kept a low profile across the field, and hiked out to the car.

Things continued this way for a while. Several nights a week, Butch and I made our way to the now familiar old shed and watched the activity. One of the things we were surprised to see was that the gang was racially integrated, an unusual thing with outlaw bikers in those days. As people came and went under the porch light there was one very dark-complected man who was nearly always present. When the U-Haul van showed up, it always seemed to cause a flurry of excitement. Compared to surveillances I helped with later in my career, this was completely unsophisticated and fairly dangerous. We had no kind of communication with the outside world, no portable radios, no cell phones. Whatever happened, it was up to us to handle.

The theory that we developed was that a crew, using the van, was bringing in motorcycles at night and putting them into the barn. It was not a stretch of imagination to suppose that these bikes were stolen. We couldn't get near enough to watch the place in the day, but it seemed logical that they were dismantling the bikes in the barn and running parts or completely trans- formed motorcycles out of there during the day.

To gather more evidence of whatever illegal activity might be going on at the farm, we looked for a way to get some photos. Neither LaBerge nor I was very skilled with photography, so he contacted Deputy Dennis Berry from the Hennepin County Sher- iff's Department and requested his help. Berry had a reputation as a techno-whiz and agreed that he would accompany us to our secret vantage point. He'd bring a 35mm camera with some fast film and might be able to capture some images of the night time activity.

It was clear and the moon was full on the night when the three of us began our hike across the field. The moonlight was so vivid that we cast shadows on the ground. A pretty good breeze blew from behind us and on toward the house. As we approached the shed and stepped over the remnants of an old foundation, a never-before-seen dog began to bark furiously at us from the backyard of the farmhouse. He ran back and forth in the yard, not quite brave enough to approach us, but doing his best to tell the world that someone was out there. It was too bright and we were too exposed to retreat, so we hit the ground behind the old foundation with just a few weeds for cover. As we did this, we saw a number of people come out of the house, alerted by the dog. They spread out and began walking across the farmyard in our direction. Some carried guns.

I pulled my revolver as the bikers moved our way and laid prone with my gun extended in front of me. Some of them were clearly going to bypass us, but one guy was walking directly toward us. With the moonlight as bright as it was, he would see us. As he got nearer, I could clearly see that he was carrying a handgun in his right hand, pointed down beside his leg. My thought was that if he saw us, he might not say anything, but just bring the gun up and take a shot. I watched him down the barrel of my pistol, determined that if his right hand came up, I would shoot him. I expected a running gun battle in the moonlit field, cops versus Outlaws.

Hyper-vigilance is hard to maintain. Even a well-trained police officer may be highly alert as he begins to search for a suspect but will relax as the search goes on with no results. So it was with the Outlaws. They began their approach in a well-formed skirmish line. As they crossed the farmyard and started into the field, they straggled and, one by one, gave up the search and turned back. With my gun locked on the chest of our main threat, I watched him slow and come to a stop about twenty feet from us. He stood for a few moments, looking intently at the spot where I lay prone, partially camouflaged by a clump of milk-weed, feet sticking out in the bright moonlight. If he had scratched his nose, I would have shot him.

Then he shrugged and turned to join the others, who had apparently decided that the dog was wrong. I normally like dogs, but they could have kicked this one for raising a false alarm with no hard feelings from me. When all of the bad guys were back in the house, we literally crawled all the way across the field. Dennis Berry's terse analysis of our surveillance effort was, "You guys sure live dangerously."

We'd have been willing to go back again on another night, but the dog's presence made it seem futile. While the detectives were trying to think of another tactic, I returned to uniform duty. Whenever I was working the east district, I drove down the river road past the farmhouse several times a shift. It wasn't unusual for squads to check the remote areas, and the bikers didn't seem alarmed as long as I just kept going on by. With some knowledge of which vehicles belonged at the farm, I could tell if anything unusual was happening there.

One Sunday morning, perhaps two weeks after the dog incident, I drove by the farm and spotted an unknown car by the house. It was early in the day, so I risked a quick stop to look at the car with binoculars and was able to identify it as a freshly reported stolen car. Once my heart stopped pounding, I headed for a pay phone at warp speed to notify LaBerge. He quickly decided to raid the farm and began putting together a team and drafting a search warrant. I was directed to pick up an unmarked squad and double up with Officer John Glynn to watch that the car didn't get away. We set up under the old Cedar Avenue Bridge, watching the only exit from the river road. By late morning everything was set, and a cavalcade of squads came rolling down the road. We dropped in the line and raced toward the farmhouse. Adrenaline is always a factor in a raid, especially an unrehearsed one such as this. We must have done seventy miles an hour down that little dirt road, braking hard and careening into the farm yard. Squad cars at crazy angles with doors standing open surrounded the house and barn. Cops ran for cover positions, racking their shotguns as they went. The captain in charge of the raid was on a bullhorn, yelling at the bikers to come out of the house with their hands up.

Out they came, six or seven bikers and one bedraggled looking girl. They hit the ground as commanded. With everyone seemingly out of the house, the captain with the bullhorn shouted, "This is your last chance to come out—anyone still in the house is coming out dead!"

He turned to Glynn and me and said, "You two guys, take the house!"

With guns drawn, Glynn and I crashed into the kitchen, then raced through the house, finding no one. A stealthy passage would have been much wiser, but we were still loaded up with adrenaline. The stench inside was nearly overwhelming. Besides general filth throughout the house, there were rotten fish on the kitchen table, carp that one of the residents must have caught in the nearby river and left without cleaning. Once we had cleared the house, we ran back outside.

It turned out we had been right about what was going on at the farm. The barn was a motorcycle chop shop with stolen bikes in various stages of disassembly. The cycles that the gang had been using, all Harley Davidsons, were also stolen. The frames had been ground and re-stamped with bogus serial numbers.

The Outlaws went to jail that day, a place where they seemed to feel at home. And the black guy? He wasn't. He just looked that way until we were close enough to see white skin in the wrinkles around his eyes where they'd been watering as he rode his bike. He was known to the outlaw biker world as "Barabbas" and apparently hadn't taken a bath in a long, long time.

9

THE STADIUM

When I was growing up, the only big time Minnesota professional sports entity was the Minneapolis Lakers Basketball Team. That changed in 1961 when the Minnesota Twins, closely followed by the Minnesota Vikings, came to town. Both groups operated, during their respective seasons, at Metropolitan Stadium at 80th and Cedar, now the site of the Mall of America in Bloomington. The stadium was a boon to us Bloomington cops in the sense that it meant more income. Every hour spent there was extra duty, paid at an overtime rate; we were the envy of neighboring police departments that would have liked a ride on the gravy train. While the money was nice, the job itself could be grueling and exhausting.

In the 1960s, Bloomington's uniformed guys rotated shifts every two weeks. Even under normal circumstances we never fully acclimated to our hours of work or sleep. When we added a chunk of five or six hours of work into the middle of our off time, it felt like burning the candle at both ends and in the middle.

The worst stretch was baseball season because of the number

of contests played compared to football. Early in the season most of the games were held in the afternoon. During a long home stand, if we were unlucky enough to be working dogwatch, we would get off at eight in the morning, go home for an hour or two of sleep, and report to the stadium by 11:00. We drew for assignments, most of them involving directing in-coming traffic, manning an area inside the stadium during the game, then presiding over the world's biggest traffic jam when things ended. If we were lucky, we might get back home by 5:30 in the afternoon so that we could try to get a little more sleep before getting back into the squad at midnight. Day after day of this routine turned us into uniformed zombies.

Cedar Avenue was a multi-lane divided highway as it passed the stadium. Directing traffic with cars bearing down at 60+ miles per hour was risky business; if you wanted to live long enough to retire, you gave it your complete attention and were ready to bail out at any moment.

The stadium's capacity was about 46,000, but baseball crowds were seldom more than half of that, making them pretty manageable. Directing motorists in was fairly simple; they were mostly sober and didn't all arrive at the same time. By about the end of the first inning, we'd leave our outside posts and go to our assigned areas inside the ballpark where we could watch the action on the field when we weren't dealing with problems that came our way. I got to see some of the great Twins players like Harmon Killebrew, Tony Oliva and Rod Carew as well as visiting baseball legends such as Willie Mays and Mickey Mantle.

While the game was going on, the beer vendors were parading up and down the aisles, lubricating the fans, preparing them for the drive home. During the eighth inning, we'd head back out to the street for the grand finale. When the game ended, people seemed to think that they should be able to get into their cars and drive straight home with no delays. As the thousands of cars crept toward one of the four parking lot exits onto Cedar Avenue, each driver held us personally responsible for the slow progress. I'm sure they all thought that they could have done a much more efficient job of directing traffic than we could; many of them rolled down their windows and expressed that feeling as they finally made the turn onto the highway and freedom. The ones we had to watch out for were the buses; many of the fans who were sober enough to get the bus windows open jeered and threw beer cans at us as they passed. Without means of communication, we just dodged any flying objects and kept waving the cars on.

Football season brought things up a few notches. In the 1960s, as far as I recall, Monday Night Football hadn't yet come into existence; all of the Vikings' games were played on Sunday afternoons in whatever kind of weather was happening that day. The mechanics were the same as those for baseball, but everything was more extreme. The crowds were capacity, the fans were more raucous and unruly, and the weather got colder and colder as the season progressed. I remember one game when the temperature was near zero Fahrenheit at kickoff time. We stood there for hours, our outdoor gear substandard by today's measurement, with the wind blasting straight from the North Pole across acres of parking lot.

Inside the stadium it wasn't much better. There was heat in the hallways and bathrooms, but the fans and players were all out in the elements. Bud Grant was the Vikings' coach at that time. He believed that real men didn't need heaters along the sidelines, so his players had to tough it out just as we did.

My favorite assignment during the game was sideline duty. That was the area where it was all happening, literally a few feet from the playing field. It was surprising how many people other than players were down in that area: coaches, officials, cheerleaders, and a host of people with no discernible roles. It seemed odd to think of me protecting monstrous guys in helmets and shoulder pads, but if there was trouble, I was ready. Mostly I watched the game. Generally, the sideline view is the worst one in the house unless something happens right in front of you; then it's spectacular.

I was standing down toward one end zone when Gene Washington, a Vikings wide receiver, sprinted past his defender and raced down the sideline. The quarterback threw a long, beautiful spiral that must have gone at least forty yards through the air. As Washington drew even with me, he looked up, the ball dropped into his hands, and he ran it in for a touchdown. One of the officials trotting down the field after the play turned to me and said, "You must have gotten a pretty good look at that one!" The receiver couldn't have been more than five feet away from me when he made the catch.

You could not only see interesting things on the field, you could hear what went on between the players, much of which didn't bear repeating. In one game the fans were mercilessly screaming at Joe Kapp, the Vikings' journeyman quarterback. Finally, after one play, Kapp walked over to the sidelines, faced the stands, raised his hand high in an obscene gesture, held the pose for about five seconds, and returned to the huddle. Nowadays I suppose he'd have been fined a vast amount and suspended for a game or two. Then it was just Joe Kapp being himself and no one thought much of it.

After the game, the exit process was slow. The people had much the same attitude as those leaving baseball games only there were many more of them. We served double duty, helping them get safely underway and providing someone to blame for their creeping progress. I quickly learned to ignore taunts, curses, and unkind suggestions; what choice did I have? I once had a good laugh at one of my critics, though. It was after a late season game, and there was deep snow in the median between the north and south bound lanes. As a car made the right turn to go toward Minneapolis, the driver rolled down his window, stuck his head out, and cursed at me. So intent was he on venting his feelings that he turned too wide and buried his car in the ditch where he and his carload remained long after everyone else was gone.

In 1967, the Minnesota North Stars hockey team came to town, playing their games in the brand-new Met Sports Center on the north side of the complex. The building only held 15,000 people, so the hockey crowds were more manageable than football. Since the games were played in mid-winter, we got the worst weather that nature had to offer as we directed traffic in and out in the dark. The only bright spot was it was too cold for people to want to roll their windows down, so we didn't have to listen to their comments as they left.

The most interesting assignment at a hockey game was penalty box duty. We'd sit in the opposing team's side of the box and watch the crowd behind that area when there was a player serving a penalty. The fans took great delight in harassing the other team's players, and some thought it was clever to reach up over the Plexiglas and pour beer on them. Close up, those hockey players were the toughest looking people I've ever seen. This was the era before players were required to wear helmets; there didn't seem to be a guy on the ice who had any teeth left, and they all had zipper marks on their faces.

Gump Worsley, one of the North Stars' goalies, was one of the last two players in the NHL to tend goal without a mask. He looked the part. One night in 1968, Bill Masterton, one of the North Stars' players, was killed when his head hit the ice during a game. I wasn't there that night, but a couple of my fellow officers rode with him in the ambulance and gave him what help they could.

Recently my wife and I visited the Mall of America. I noticed that there were Bloomington police officers everywhere, in ones or twos, watching the crowds, patrolling the hallways, doing what cops do. Everyone looks young to me these days, but I doubt that any of the ones I saw were even alive when I and my compatriots directed traffic, or fought with drunks, or watched Harmon Killebrew hit one of his monster homeruns.

I wonder if they'd like to hear about what used to go on here? I asked myself. *Probably not,* I answered, after a moment's thought. So, I just sat on a bench and waited for my wife.

10

UC

I n 1970, with five years of uniformed police work under my belt, I got a chance to embark on a new adventure. After a selection process, Jim Hessel, Roger Pedersen, and I were picked to form Bloomington's brand-new Narcotics Section. Pedersen, a few years older than Hessel and me and already a detective, was to be the unit coordinator. Hessel and I were going "UC," police jargon for undercover.

At the tail end of the 1960s and the beginning of the 70s, the whole drug thing was coming on with a rush. Vietnam War protestors, hippies, and narcotics dealers merged into an amalgam of violence and drugs that we hadn't previously seen. Police departments across the country reacted with stepped-up enforcement. In the Twin Cities, a number of agencies banded together to form the Metro Area Narcotics Squad (MANS). Hessel, Pedersen, and I were deputized and assigned to that unit.

To me, the most interesting part of a police undercover operation is the chance to become "one of them." By assuming the identity of a lawbreaker and rubbing shoulders with others of that ilk on their turf, I saw crime from the inside out, a strange sensation for a straightlaced cop. To move around in that world of drug use, sexual promiscuity, dishonesty, and, sometimes, treachery, and remain unstained is the ultimate challenge.

The costume of the day in the drug world was long hair, flowered shirts, bell-bottom jeans, and military jackets. A visit to the Salvation Army Store took care of our clothing needs. The hair took more time, but it wasn't very long before I looked disreputable enough that store clerks began to look at me with a wary eye.

The assignment for us narcotics neophytes was simple and direct: Seize dope, arrest dope dealers. We worked with informants, some of whom were willing to introduce us to their dealer/sources. If our story sounded good to the dealer, we'd buy drugs, set up future transactions without the informant, and eventually do a "buy-bust" of the dealer. Alternatively, there were some dope havens in the Twin Cities where the dealers felt so safe that anyone who looked the part could buy drugs without references. The West Bank area in Minneapolis was one of those places. On a sunny day, there were hippies everywhere, smoking pot in People's Park, wandering stoned along Cedar Avenue, or looking for someone who was "holding," slang for a person with dope to sell. There was a railing that ran along the side of Richter's Drug Store where the dealers stood and sold drugs to people who lined up to buy from them. One guy might sell acid, another speed, another hash. Once when I was there, a guy was walking back and forth hollering "Lids," holding a baggie of marijuana in the air, like a vendor selling hotdogs at a ball game. Buying drugs in that setting was easy. The hard part was identifying the dealer for future arrest.

In later years, I worked undercover in some pretty sophisticated operations with a lot of back-up and high-tech surveillance help. In these early days the whole covert operation game was new to us. We worked with minimal equipment and learned as we went. I carried a .380 caliber Walther PPKS semi-auto pistol and often worked with no one watching my

back or even knowing where I was. Later, as a narcotics supervisor, I never would have allowed one of my agents to do that,
but, at the time, we didn't know any better. I might go with an
informant into a house full of hippies, never knowing for sure
if the "snitch" was playing it straight or double crossing me.
We'd have a story about who I was and how we knew each
other. I always had to have a plausible reason why, even though
I was looking for drugs, I couldn't use any while I was there.
Usually, I had some place I had to get to, so, even though I told
them I would love to get high with them, I couldn't do it right
then.

Just about every place I went into had some kind of drugs.
Once in a while I would stumble onto the mother lode. One time
we had arrested a low-level drug dealer and convinced him to
give us his supplier in return for leniency, a common trade-off in
the drug enforcement world. He gave me a gold-plated introduc-
tion to a dealer named Mike who lived just off Lake Street and
Nicollet Avenue in Minneapolis. When I walked into Mike's
house, I saw more dope than I'd ever seen at one time. The
kitchen table was completely covered with bags of pot, packages
of brown-and-clears (pharmaceutical speed) and other drugs I
couldn't look at closely enough to identify. I made my drug
purchase and left. I made a follow-up buy a few days later, but
before we could get our case together and arrest Mike, he was
shot in a drug rip-off. I never heard whether Minneapolis PD
made a case on the shooter.

Often, we made a drug buy, and, if we didn't see any possibility of going any further with the case, we busted the crooks
right on the spot. Those situations could get pretty wild sometimes. One night, Officer Dennis Sigafoos and I went into a
house in North Minneapolis where we bought a pound of pot,
then pulled our guns and tinned (displayed our badges to) the
five or six people there. Pandemonium broke out: One of the
men, who was high, ran at me screaming. I leveled my gun at his

face, yelling, "Freeze or I'll kill you!" I must have had the trigger partially squeezed when he stopped and backed up.

Meanwhile, one of the women bolted for a back bedroom, chased by Sigafoos. I could hear them screaming and fighting but couldn't do anything but cover the rest of the bunch in the living room. It turned out that she had grabbed a loaded shotgun, but Sigafoos was able to wrestle it away from her and put her down before she could shoot.

One bit of fallout from the arrest that Sigafoos and I made was that our names and descriptions were printed in *Hundred Flowers*, a counter-culture newspaper. The information had been submitted by the woman we'd arrested. It was comical when I went to the West Bank to get a souvenir copy of the paper. I walked down Cedar Avenue, passing people who were reading my description with no clue that one of the hated subjects of the article was ten feet away.

One of our other arrest techniques was to attend rock concerts and watch people selling drugs. This was risky because when we tried to make an arrest, the crowd could turn against us. One night Hessel and I sat a few rows behind a guy who looked to be dealing pretty big time. We knew it would be hard to pinch him and get him out of the arena, so we waited until the concert was over and, when he was near one of the exits, grabbed him and told him he was under arrest. The plan was to drag him quickly out through the exit, but he put up a fight and started screaming, "Help! Narcs!" We were mobbed by hippies, who tore him out of our grasp and pummeled us pretty badly. We were glad to get out of the place intact. Through some good police work, we were able to identify the guy and put him down at an apartment in Northeast Minneapolis. A couple of nights later, with arrest warrant in hand, we visited the suspect in his apartment, and justice, belatedly, prevailed. The worst thing about the rock concert idea was that we couldn't hear anything for about three days after we'd been there.

We often joined forces with other narcotics officers for drug raids. We normally went with a no-knock search warrant, justified by the ease with which dope can be flushed down the toilet if you have to wait for the dealer to open the door. We had no body armor or any other special equipment for breaching doors. We just yelled, "Police," kicked in the door, and went in like gangbusters. Once in a while, things didn't work quite that smoothly. I went on one raid where the leading agent ran up to the back door, gave it a good kick, and just bounced off. He kicked again, same result. With more and more determination he kept kicking the door, which didn't give a bit. In spite of whatever danger might have lurked inside, and the adrenaline surge that fueled a dynamic entry, we were overcome by the humor of the situation. As he continued his efforts, we began to chant the number of each kick: "Seven! Eight! Nine! Ten!" He was up to about fifteen when a couple of Minneapolis cops, who had simultaneously gone in through the front door, came to the back and let us in.

Sometimes, when we didn't have information to go after specific drug dealers, we still messed with them. The dopers were always poised to flush their drugs when they thought the cops were coming. Any night of the week, we could go into one of the ramshackle apartment buildings in Minneapolis, pound on the wall, shout, "Police," and hear ten toilets flush simultaneously. Imagine the suspense and confusion in the ten apartments when a surge of pot, speed, LSD, and cocaine made its way to the Mississippi River and no one ever came to the door.

Looking back, one of the remarkable things about that era of law enforcement was that no one ever doubted my word (nor should they have). I could go out by myself and buy dope from a suspect and later get an arrest warrant for him. When we got to court, he could have five witnesses come in and lie for him, and the jury would still believe me. That's because, in spite of the hatred the hippies had for us, the rest of the world saw cops as the good guys. That all changed after Watergate, when the public began to view the government as a sinister force. It didn't take defense attorneys long to learn to play on that in every closing argument, and things have not been the same since.

Those were heady times for a twenty-seven-year-old police officer. Night after night, we bought dope or kicked in doors, risking our necks in chancy undercover situations or arresting violent crazy people. I loved the heart-pumping action, but was also wise enough to see that the job was not altogether good for me. I was married with two small kids; being out every night didn't serve well in my role as a husband or father. Spending most of my working hours with dope dealers, snitches, prostitutes, and a host of other unsavory characters made me tougher and gave me a harder outlook on life than before. I made some bad enemies through some of my arrests and worried about the vulnerability of my family. We had a German shepherd in the house, and I slept with a loaded gun on the nightstand. In June 1971, I left the police department and was out of the business for a couple of years. I got back into it in 1973 and worked some different and even more dangerous undercover assignments, but that's for another chapter.

And why did Liz, my wife, put up with all of this? I don't know, but she's made of good stuff.

11

UNDERCOVER 2.0

I n 1973, after a two-and-one-half year hiatus from the police business, I returned to the vocation that would account for the next thirty years of my working life. I had received a phone call from former Bloomington Officer Bruce Jones, who told me that he now was an agent with the Organized Crime Intelligence Unit, a Minnesota state organization operating under the authority of the Attorney General. He explained that one of his unit's agents had just resigned and a replacement was needed. I was flattered to hear that he'd immediately thought of me. After meeting with Jones' boss and learning more about the OCIU, it was a pretty simple decision to get back into the game.

When I joined it, the OCIU was a tiny organization with four agents, an intelligence analyst, and two secretaries. Its assignment, a delightful one, could be summed up in three words: "Catch big crooks." We worked with many people from other enforcement agencies. The luxury we had that made us different from most detectives and federal agents with whom we worked was our lack of reactive caseloads—no stacks of unsolved robberies or burglaries on our desks, just the freedom to pursue some of the significant and prosperous folks in our community who had found, so far, that crime did pay. The unit had just come off a real triumph, having successfully done a wiretap investigation of a bigtime criminal operation that had seemed untouchable to traditional police methods.

I hadn't been a state employee for very long when my past experience as an undercover narcotics agent came into play. Jones had an informant, an old gangster, who told him of three brothers in Minneapolis who were accomplished stick-up men and burglars. If Jones could provide a telephone number and an undercover agent to play the part, the informant was willing to pass the phone number to his friends as a possible outlet for stolen property. Of course, I was elected to play the part of the fence.

We had an undercover phone line in our office, and within a few days, I got a call from "Lyle" who said he was a friend of "Joe." Lyle said he had thirteen IBM Selectric Ball typewriters for sale. Today you couldn't give an IBM Selectric away, but then they were state-of-the-art. We settled on a price, he gave me the address of a cheap apartment in South Minneapolis, and I agreed to make the purchase that afternoon. We had no budget for undercover transactions at that time, so it would have to be a buy-bust.

Late that afternoon, with several OCIU agents and Minneapolis cops covering, I drove a Dodge delivery van, usually used for surveillance, into the apartment lot. One of the improvements in the undercover world since my narcotics days was the availability of hidden transmitters—body bugs. They were temperamental and didn't have much range, but there was, at least, a chance that the covering officers would be able to listen to what was going on and either make an arrest or come to my rescue. The plan was to start loading the typewriters into the van, whereupon the backup officers would swoop in.

I usually didn't feel very nervous when approaching a UC

deal. "On guard" or "watchful" would better describe my state as
I climbed the stairs and knocked on the apartment door. I was
thinking about the informant's description of the brothers as
armed robbers, and it certainly occurred to me that they could be
setting me up for a robbery. It was a relief when Lyle answered
the door, introduced me to his two brothers, gestured to a pile of
boxes in the living room and said, "Let's start loading them up."
After a quick verification that there were typewriters, as
described, in the cartons, the brothers began carrying them down
to the van.

One of the problems with arresting multiple suspects in a
fluid situation is that it's difficult to get all of the players to the
right place at the right time. Lyle and I each carried a box down
to the van with his brothers straggling along behind, also
carrying boxes. By the time the brothers were out by the van,
Lyle had gone back into the building for his second load. The
backup cops swooped in and arrested the brothers, with the
commotion that was always part of those affairs, but Lyle was
nowhere in sight. Afraid that he may have heard the arrests going
down or seen the action through the window, I pulled my gun
and raced into the building and up the stairs. There on the
landing was Lyle, carrying box number two, oblivious to the
action in the parking lot.

"Hold it, Lyle! I'm a cop!" I shouted as I leveled my .357 at
him from about six stairs down. He stood there, frozen. After a
long ten seconds, he carefully set the box down and raised his
hands. From then on, whenever they needed someone to play any
kind of UC role, they somehow decided I was the guy.

In 1975, the OCIU was transferred to the Bureau of Criminal Apprehension (BCA), a much bigger organization with a
strong reputation. Our mission remained about the same, but
our resources were greatly increased. In the late '70s, we
started doing sting operations -- moving into an area, representing ourselves as stolen property fences. Things often

started slowly, then picked up speed as each crook with whom we had done business would vouch for us to his friends. This sometimes would go on for eight or nine months as we bought stolen property and cataloged the evidence but waited until we could arrest a number of defendants at the same time. I did a lot of the undercover work in these operations and quickly learned to wheel and deal with the crooks. It was much easier dealing with thieves and robbers than it had been with dope dealers. This group tended to be down to business and usually did what they said they'd do. In the drug world, no one is reliable, and about half of the deals one tries to set up never happen.

The officers who worked together, either undercover or providing back up, were a serious, tight-knit group, but sometimes things happened that cracked us up. One night Agent John Fossum and I were covering Agent Dan Boykin, who had worked his way into an auto theft ring. He was meeting a couple of future defendants at an Embers Restaurant, where he was to take a look at a stolen car they had for sale. In case he decided to buy the car, Boykin had brought along a brand-new agent to drive it away. Boykin's instructions to the agent were specific: "Don't say anything, just come along with me and do what I tell you." As we listened to the meeting on the bug, we suddenly heard Boykin say, "Put that away! You don't need that here!" Simultaneously we heard one of the crooks say, "Hey, man, is this guy a cop?" The new man was so nervous about meeting with criminals that he had slipped his gun out from his waistband and put it on his lap under the table, from whence it eventually clattered onto the floor, causing a brief sensation. Like any good UC guy, Boykin just kept on talking, settled the crooks down, and did the deal. On our way back to the office, Fossum and I fulfilled our solemn responsibility to draw from the situation a proper nickname for the new agent. Magnum PI was a popular TV detective show at that time, and, from that evening until he retired, that particular agent was known to everyone at the BCA as "Magnum."

A mistake that some cops make when working undercover is to put on too much of an act. I found the best and simplest thing to do was to be myself and just add the things that were necessary to the role I played. I'm an even-tempered guy who doesn't drink or smoke. As a cop I became familiar with every profane term then in fashion, but I didn't need them to express myself. To members of the underworld, I was a nice guy who didn't seem to have any vices other than a willingness to make a dishonest buck. They were fine with that. I know the construction business, so that's what I represented as my main vocation.

Some of the time I had the luxury of working with a partner. One of my favorites in those days was BCA Agent Paul Gerber. To the people we dealt with, we must have seemed the oddest pairing they'd ever encountered. A reporter who interviewed us one time for a newspaper article described Gerber this way: "He's a character, hyper and flamboyant, the kind of guy whose raucous, jovial voice dominates a noisy bar." He went on to write, "Terry Smith is quite the opposite. Dark haired, with a little grey in his beard, he's a somber, pensive sort." As partners we complemented each other. Gerber stood out in a crowd, connected easily with people, and behaved outrageously enough that no one ever suspected him of being a cop. I kept track of details, remembered what we had done with the evidence, and kept an eye on what was happening away from the action while Paul was "on stage." I liked working with him because his heart was in it, he was effective, and I always trusted him to stick with me no matter what happened.

There's hardly any job in law enforcement that doesn't involve some danger. I've always felt that the uniformed cop is in the most dangerous of all police assignments. Everyone knows who he is, and he often doesn't know where a threat will come from. Undercover work, though, calls for a particular type of bravery (some would say recklessness). There is no doubt that some of the bad guys with whom we interacted would have tried to kill us if they'd known who we were. We went to dangerous places: houses or apartments controlled by the crooks, tough bars where twenty people could turn on us if they made us as cops, out-of-the-way-locations where the seller wanted to meet us to be safe from prying eyes (or to set us up for execution if he'd figured out who we really were). We did all of this knowing that the bug might not work, our back-up cover team might lose us, or an attack might come so quickly that we'd be on our own to deal with it. A gift of gab and a concealed .357 magnum were the tools upon which I counted the most.

To my knowledge, the closest I came to losing my life in an undercover deal was in Duluth, Minnesota, in 1979. Duluth Officers Gary Waller and Dave Cismoski had made a case on an oft-convicted felon who knew he was going back to the joint on his current beef (a little cop slang there) if he didn't cooperate with them. They had so much leverage that he decided to take the ultimate risk for a crook, turn informant and burn some of his criminal associates by introducing them to a UC cop. The possibilities with this informant made the cops starry-eyed. He ran with a gang of very professional burglars and armed robbers who were thought to be responsible for crimes across Minnesota and Wisconsin. He knew of two who were holding about twenty expensive guns, taken in a recent burglary, and looking for a buyer. He told the Duluth detectives that he could only introduce one person and that the UC had better not carry a gun or wear a bug because the bad guys would search him. I agreed to go in on these terms, although not without serious second thoughts. I met with the informant and told him to set up a meeting with the suspects.

The next evening, I walked up the steps to the informant's front door—no bug, no gun, covered by four cops who could only park way down the street and watch the house with binoculars. I had told them that if things got deadly inside the house, I would try to throw something out through the front picture window or take a dive through myself if I could. I knocked, walked in to a "Come in," and found the informant and two other men sitting, watching TV. It was awkward because no one acknowledged me at first. The informant seemed to be speechless, probably thinking, "What have I done?"

The other two simply ignored me until I finally said, "Well, let's get it on." The informant introduced me to "Rick" and "Dennis," who then looked at me for the first time. Dennis seemed to be the friendlier one. Rick was good-sized, very tough looking, surly and skeptical, and clearly the leader. In a fight, I probably couldn't have taken either of them, certainly not both at the same time. Rick questioned me closely as to who I was, how long I had known the informant, and what our past relationship had been. No problem here because we'd gone over all of this in advance; if the informant could remember his lines, he'd have given the same story when setting up the deal.

After we'd discussed things for about five minutes, Rick said, "We've got to talk." The three went into the kitchen. A few minutes later they came back to where I was watching TV and Rick said, "OK, we'll do business."

In the criminal world, there may be honor among some thieves, but there's a lot of treachery, too. What these guys wanted was my money. If they could get it without giving me the guns, so much the better for them. They presumed that I knew that and wouldn't be stupid enough to have carried the money along with me. They knew I wanted the guns and believed that, if I could get them without paying for them, I would. They also knew that I could be a cop. With this mutual understanding, we did the little dance that was part of all of these deals, negotiating on the mechanics of delivering the guns and handing over the money. We agreed that they would go and get the guns and would call the informant's house in a short time to say where they would meet me to complete the deal. I would be prepared to get the money to them once I had seen the guns.

I waited with the informant, expecting a phone call, and was surprised a short time later to hear a knock on the door. Rick and Dennis had changed the plan, I'm sure to throw me a curve, and simply showed up again. They told me I should go and look in the back of my van, which was parked in front of the house, then come back inside. Doing so, I found a couple of sacks of long guns, all brand new. We'd already agreed on a price, so I got my money from where it was hidden and went back inside to pay them. Rick told me to give the money to the informant. This was typical strategy for crooks. The thinking was that, if I was a cop and the guy who introduced me was a snitch, then they'd later claim that it was the snitch who sold me the guns, not them.

I countered by saying, "I don't care who gets the money, but I want you to watch me count it out so there's no argument about how much I paid." Then, turning my back on the informant, I counted out the bills onto an end table with Rick watching intently.

It was a relief to walk out of the house. I was even more relieved the following day when I had a chance to talk with the informant.

"What did they talk about in the kitchen?" I asked him.

His reply: "Rick thought that you were a cop and he wanted to come back and kill you. Dennis talked him out of it."

During the next couple of months, we turned those guys inside out. When I heard that Dennis had been hospitalized for a drug overdose, I went to see him as he was recovering in the hospital. I told him I didn't like dealing with Rick because he made me nervous (partly true). If Dennis could introduce me over the phone to someone else in his line of work, I'd pay him $50. A few days later, Dennis hooked me up with "John," who had some chainsaws for sale. In the ensuing weeks, I bought the chainsaws and a vanload of stolen stereo gear taken from a

Duluth electronics store. I also had several very interesting and instructive visits with John about how they pulled their burglaries and future jobs they planned. I was secretly amused when he told me that one of the things he liked most about his work was the thrill of danger and excitement. *Just like me*, I thought, *only on the other side of the action.*

As the time to shut down our operation neared, we worked to cut down the chances for encountering violence when arresting this group. To disarm them, I told John I was looking for guns to rent for a big job coming up—I couldn't talk about what it was, but he'd be able to read about it in the paper. He said he could help me out and, a few days later, brought me several guns, including two sawed-off shotguns. Our arrest plans had to be fast-tracked when John breathlessly called me to say they had just burglarized a West Duluth ski shop, cleaning out the entire inventory of Nordic skis. They had them stashed in a stolen van and needed to unload them right away. We agreed to meet at John's place that evening.

Just after dark I pulled into the parking lot of John's apartment building, wearing a bug, carrying a gun, covered by an arrest team of cops and "Joe," Duluth's most ferocious police dog. The plan was, if anyone ran, we would all stop, and Joe would go after the runner. I was greeted at the apartment door by John and Rick, who was, this time, friendly. They had me back my truck up to a garage stall in the complex, and we moved about two hundred skis from van to van. They said they were having trouble getting the stolen van started and needed to get it out of there. I agreed to park my van off to the side and come back to see if I could help them. As I did this, I gave the arrest signal and, within moments, several squads came swooping in. For the next several minutes, the action was wild. As the cops were leaping out of their cars, I heard a furious battering, smashing sound at the front of the garage and thought, *They're breaking right out through the wall!* Pulling my gun, I raced around to the other side of the garage but found nothing happening there. Meanwhile, Rick had charged out of the dark garage and right through the cops before they could react. As he raced away across a field, we all did what we were supposed to: We stopped and Joe went after him. We heard Rick scream as the dog nailed him -- then nothing. Meanwhile, most of the cops had started after Rick, so I went back to the front of the garage just as John came running out.

"Hold it, John! I'm a cop!" I yelled. He skidded to a stop with his hands up. Moments later, Joe's handler returned, saying that Rick had gotten away. Joe had grabbed his wrist, as trained, but Rick had begun battering the dog on the head with his fist until the dog let go and wouldn't go back on the attack. The dog handler, running to catch up with the action, went to draw his gun and found that it had fallen out of his holster as he ran. After the adrenaline had worn off, Rick realized that his goose had been thoroughly cooked and gave himself up several days later.

The sharpest burst of fear I ever felt in a UC situation was during the arrest of an evil little guy who had hired me to kill his wife. A smalltown Chief of Police had been contacted by an informant who said that a co-worker had approached him, asking if the informant would do "something serious" for a good pay-off. When it came out that the man was looking for someone to murder his wife, the informant said he wouldn't do it, but might be able to find someone who would. When the Chief heard the story, he went straight to the resident BCA Agent, who contacted me. I had two meetings with the man, all on tape, in which he told me how much he hated his wife and that he wanted her to suffer as much as possible as she died. We agreed on a price and arranged for payment.

The second meeting was in a motel room. There was an arrest team of two BCA Agents and the Chief listening and recording in the next room. At a verbal signal from me, they would station themselves in the hallway and arrest the perpetrator as we left the room. When I felt that the case had been completed, I told the man that it would all be taken care of in the next few days.

He said, "You don't know how good that makes me feel." As we stood to leave the room, I gave the arrest signal, expecting just to lay hands on the guy as he preceded me through the door. Instead, as the door swung open, I was confronted by the sight of the Chief in combat crouch position, his gun leveled shakily at the defendant, who was, of course, directly in front of me. "Freeeeeze," he screamed, in a voice about two octaves higher than normal. We did.

By the early 1980s, I had moved on to other assignments. Even though I had liked living on the edge, I felt less and less inclined to take the kinds of risks that could have left behind a lovely widow and four orphans. But here's what I liked least about undercover work: lying. I know that I was playing a role, as an actor does, but it never felt quite right to me to look someone in the eye and tell him something that wasn't true. I hate dishonesty in any form, and it was almost scary to find out how good I was at conning people. Realizing this, I have worked hard at being scrupulously truthful since I snookered my last criminal.

12

SURVEILLANCE

We did a lot of dangerous driving over the years—pursuing suspects, responding to emergencies, rushing to help officers in trouble. The riskiest car travel in my line of work was driving while on surveillance. When I was in the Organized Crime Unit, following criminals was a daily occurrence. We had a good idea who most of our major offenders were. Watching where they went and who they met was basic to understanding what they were up to and where they might be vulnerable. Of course, the idea was to do this without their realizing we were on them, a good trick with people who looked in their rearview mirrors as much as they looked forward. We'd use four or five nondescript cars and would frequently switch off positions so the subject wouldn't see the same car behind him for more than a few blocks. The "eyeball" driver would keep up a running narrative on the radio, and the other cars would scramble to position themselves for what might happen as the secret pursuit continued.

It might sound this way: "He's coming to a red light at Lake Street. I'm two behind him—looks like he's watching his mirrors a lot. The light flipped, he's continuing south. He took a quick right on 31st without signaling! I've gotta go straight!"

"Twenty-three, I'm parallel a block west, I should be able to pick him up when he comes by me." As this was happening, the other cars were racing to position themselves for whatever happened next. When the suspect vehicle came to a stop somewhere, one of the followers would try to find a position from which to watch what happened while the others would set themselves to be able to go with the car when it left. The car we were following might leave in five minutes or it might remain there for the night. At some point, the team leader would have to decide whether to keep watching or shut things down. While all of this was happening, one of the team members was noting every detail of the subject's travels and would later write a surveillance report.

Moving surveillance is tricky, as the crew tries to keep the object of the investigation from noticing anything unusual. What's harder is to do stationary surveillance from a car. One can only pull up and sit for so long before people from the neighborhood begin to notice him and wonder what he's up to. More than once, someone called the police to report that one of our surveillance units was acting suspiciously. It's not good to have a marked squad car show up in the middle of a covert operation.

We learned a few tricks to help with this problem. One was to do something that seemed normal and non-threatening to those who might notice us. Once I wanted to watch activity at a house in a residential neighborhood. Noting that there was a carwash just down the street, I washed my car, got a can of car wax, and parked under a tree directly across from the house in question. There I polished my car and watched suspects come and go. They paid no attention to the guy fifty feet away. I put about four coats of wax on the car before feeling it was time to move on. My car never looked better.

Sometimes one of us did a casual walk-by. On one

surveillance, one of our female agents and I left our cars and strolled together down the side of the street. We sat down on a low wall along the sidewalk, seemingly having a casual conversation while maintaining watch on the car we'd been following. This worked beautifully until the lady who owned the house with the wall stepped out and began screaming at us to get away from her yard. We did.

We had a van that could accommodate several people on watch from its curtained-off rear area. Typically, the watchers would be in back and another agent would park the van and walk away. This worked well but didn't fool everyone. Once, two other agents and I used the van to videotape some outlaw bikers coming and going from a bar. For some reason, the suspects became suspicious of the van and came over for a closer look. We spent several minutes huddled on the floor of the van, barely breathing, while the bikers attempted to peer into the windows and tried all of the doors before finally going back to what they had been doing.

It's one thing to follow someone just to gain information about what they might be up to; another, to track potentially violent people who may do something that requires instant police intervention. We were always well armed and ready to confront, arrest, shoot, whatever the situation might call for. We followed a couple of armed robbery suspects one night as they appeared to be casing places to rob. Finally, at a bar, it looked as if it was about to happen. One of the crooks took something from the car's trunk and they both went in. We scrambled for vantage points and prepared to take them down after they left the crowded parking lot. Then—nothing happened. They came out moments later, apparently not liking what they had found inside, and drove off.

We never knew where a surveillance would take us. One snowy winter morning, we set up on a bigtime professional shoplifter, thinking we might see him head for one of our many shopping centers in the Minneapolis-St. Paul area. He and a woman, unknown to us, followed the freeway system through Minneapolis and headed west on US 94. As they continued on past the outer suburban ring, it became apparent that we were on a road trip. It began to snow and blow fairly heavily, limiting his ability to see in the rearview mirror. That helped us, but also made driving more hazardous. It was a white-knuckle drive as the suspect held about 75 miles per hour, much too fast for the conditions. Finally, 192 miles later, they took the off ramp at Fergus Falls, Minnesota, and pulled into the mall parking lot. Both the man and woman were wearing long overcoats as they left the car and walked into the shopping center.

We'd learned from previous experience that it's actually very difficult to watch professional boosters (shoplifters) in the stores. If they feel someone's paying too much attention to them, they'll just abort the mission and leave. Instead, we set up on their car to watch their actions when they came out. It wasn't long until they exited the mall—the woman, with both hands in her coat pockets, looking about nine-and-a-half months pregnant. I videotaped them as they took a number of clothing items out from under their coats and put them in plastic garbage bags in the trunk of the car. During the next fifteen minutes or so, they moved the car to parking places near different mall entrances and repeated the performance. After completing several such trips, they got into the car and drove out of the lot in the direction of the freeway. Assuming that they'd now head back to the Twin Cities, I was getting ready to whistle up a state trooper in a marked car to help us stop and arrest them when, to everyone's amazement, they turned west onto 94, continuing our journey to points unknown.

The next community of any size is the Fargo-Moorhead area about sixty miles down the road. The Red River between those two towns is the Minnesota-North Dakota border. Knowing that we may be heading for another state where we had no police jurisdiction, we dialed up one of our acquaintants on the

Moorhead Police Department and asked him to have a crew ready to join our effort and to line up a contingent of Fargo officers as well. About an hour later, we all rolled into the West Acres Mall in Fargo where the two shoplifters continued with their routine. Finally, after they'd taken half-a-dozen loads of what looked like mostly clothing items out of the mall, the suspects got into their car and began to drive out of the lot. It must have startled the other shoppers in the main parking lot entrance to see five or six unmarked cars swoop in, surrounding and blocking the criminals' car. The male shoplifter, who had a reputation as a tough guy, seemed initially inclined to put up a fight. Moments later, face down on the concrete with a large Moorhead officer snapping on the handcuffs, he was much more docile. His partner in crime turned out to be a stripper from the Twin Cities. She was not feisty at all and put all of her energy into flirting with the Fargo cops while she was being booked. As the evening wore on, we got a search warrant for the car and found about $4,000 worth of stolen high-end clothing in plastic bags in the trunk. When the dust had settled, I called my wife to tell her I was in Fargo and wouldn't be home until the next day. She took the news in stride; this was the way a lot of our days ended.

One kind of surveillance that could be quite stressful was when we provided backup for an undercover agent. The agent was in a vulnerable spot, probably outnumbered, sometimes with violent people. If he needed rescuing, it was up to his covering officers. It was not so bad if things were going down in a fixed location. It was much more difficult if it was happening in a moving vehicle. Even if the undercover person was wearing a bug, the reception could be spotty.

Sometimes it was hard to interpret what was taking place based on what came over the bug. One Sunday afternoon, several of our people were backing up two undercover agents who were buying stolen property from some burglars. The action was taking place in a back yard where it was impossible to get a view of what was happening.

Suddenly, one of the undercover guys said, "What's he doing?"

They heard one of the crooks in the background say, "Up, up, up!" It took a minute or so for the covering officers to conclude that the UC guys were in trouble. As the backups were getting ready to swoop in, they heard that things had calmed down; the UC guys just kept on talking and were able to get the suspicious burglar, who had pulled a gun on them, to put it away. After the deal was over and the agents all got together, there was some solemn reflection on how things might have ended.

It wasn't always tense and sober, though. Sometimes unexpected things came up and brought a little humor into the scenario. In one case, a UC agent was buying stolen property from a suspect. They had an initial meeting and agreed that the crook would go and get the items he had for sale and would return directly with the property. Our mission was to follow the suspect, find where he kept his stash, let him return to consummate the deal, and then hit his storehouse with a search warrant. We followed the bad guy away, down Central Avenue in northeast Minneapolis. After about ten blocks, he pulled over to the side of the street and stopped. *What's he doing, checking for surveillance?* we wondered. Our question was answered when he got out, raised the hood of his car, and began doing what people do when their cars break down. *Oh, no, we'll be stuck here watching this guy mess with his car all day,* we thought. Then I had a bright idea. *I know something about mechanics. Maybe I can help him get going again.*

Parking on a side street, I got out and walked out to Central Avenue, then strolled along by the car. "Having car trouble?" I asked.

Soon the crook and I were both leaning under the hood, checking wires and hoses, isolating the problem. "Try it now," I said, after finding and tightening a loose battery cable. When the car started right up, the criminal jumped out and shook my hand, thanking me profusely. As he drove off, I walked around the block and got back into my car to join the surveillance once more in progress.

One other type of surveillance that we did from time to time was a stake-out. In this situation, we watched a known location for expected activity that would most likely result in an arrest. Sometimes we were there because of informant information, sometimes just from good intelligence gathering. Often nothing happened; at other times, things just didn't go as we had planned.

Early one morning, Agent John Edwards and I sat in his unmarked car, watching a vehicle parked along a street just off the frontage road of Highway 94 near Dale Street in St. Paul. Edwards had a felony arrest warrant for the car's owner. He'd developed information that the suspect was spending nights with a girlfriend in one of several apartment buildings along the street. Edwards would recognize the suspect as he approached the car, and we'd move in and make the arrest before he could drive off. The first part of the plan went off as envisioned. About eight in the morning, my partner said, "There he is!" as a young man carrying a cup of coffee approached the car. From about a half block away, we pulled out and began driving toward the car. The suspect's hand reached for his door handle. Edwards hit the gas and raced toward the target. As we slid to a stop, the suspect's eyes got big, the coffee cup went up in the air, and our quarry whirled and ran. We bailed out and chased him down the sidewalk.

I must pause for a moment to tell you about my partner. John was a good agent, tough and fearless, formerly an athlete, never one to do less than his part in a confrontation. However, it had been a long time since he'd run the hundred-yard dash. About fifteen or twenty seconds into our spirited footrace, I heard him gasp from somewhere behind me.

"I'll go back—and get—the car." From that point on, I knew it was just me and a fleeing felon.

I chased him into one of the dingy apartment buildings that lined the street, through the halls, around a few corners, and out the back door. I gained on the suspect in the straightaways but had to slow down for the corners in case he tried to ambush me as I made the turn. As we got outside, he raced toward 94 with a fifty-foot lead. I almost got him as he climbed over the freeway fence, but he was just able to evade my grasp as he dropped over onto the other side.

I've encountered a lot of people who didn't want to go to jail, but this guy was crazy. The freeway at this point was the main artery between St. Paul and Minneapolis, three lanes each way, nobody going slower than 60 mph. He ran right across the highway with cars screeching, honking, and swerving to avoid him. Not being an absolute fool, I didn't follow him. Instead, I ran the short distance to the Dale Street bridge and crossed to the other side, arriving about the time he was starting to climb the fence. Seeing me, he turned and ran back the way he had come. We did this cat and mouse thing four times back and forth across the freeway before he hit on the idea of running along the highway instead of across it. While this happened, I heard sirens coming from everywhere. Edwards had summoned help from St. Paul's finest, but no one knew exactly where we were and I had no way to communicate with them. I ran down the entrance ramp to continue the foot chase when something happened that completely took the wind out of my sails: a car pulled up beside the suspect, he jumped in, and there I was, standing along the freeway, friendless and alone. All hope was not lost, though. John Edwards had indeed gone back for the car and he pulled up beside me. We roared off after the car, catching up and running it off the road as it went up the Lexington ramp. The suspect leaped out and began to run again, but a couple of St. Paul cops with fresh legs ran him down and tackled him. I felt great satisfaction in seeing him, handcuffed in the back of a squad car. The guy who had picked him up along the freeway insisted that he didn't know the man, just thought he was "a guy in trouble." We believed him and didn't hassle him further.

One of the successful stakeouts we did was at a brand-new, just-ready-to-be-opened high school in Apple Valley, Minnesota. We'd received information from an informant that a gang of burglars was planning to break into the building overnight and steal all of the just-installed computer equipment. We borrowed a motor home and got permission to park it in a driveway across from the main school parking lot. That was our vantage point for watching the part of the building the burglars would most likely enter. We had officers in cars at strategic points, keeping an eye on traffic in the area, poised to sweep in and make an arrest.

Nothing drags on slower than an all-night surveillance. The guys in the motorhome had at least a little excitement, as an unsuspecting neighbor established a pattern of stepping out onto the back porch in her nightgown every few hours to let her seemingly incontinent dog take a series of bathroom breaks. Then about four o'clock in the morning, all attention was focused on a van that pulled into the parking lot and up by the building. As the cops watched, three men got out, pried open a door, and entered the building. Now everyone was wide awake.

The surveillance cars tightened up, ready to make the pinch. The lady with the dog could have done a flamenco dance in her yard without drawing attention from the RV. Our plan was to take the burglars down when they were back in the van and ready to leave.

How long does it take to burgle a high school? Apparently longer than one would think. Fifteen minutes turned into twenty, then thirty, and there was no sign of anyone coming out. The sun was just starting to cast a glimmer on the horizon when the plot took a nerve-wracking twist. A female jogger appeared from the darkness and began to run across the parking lot. As if following a homing beacon, she headed straight toward the corner of the building where the burglars' vehicle was parked. Completely oblivious to the van or the pried-open door just a few feet away, she proceeded to do a series of leisurely stretching exercises against the wall. Now, instead of a well-controlled arrest scenario, we had a situation that could spin out of control and was fraught with danger for the clueless woman. If the burglars came out while she was there, no one could predict what they might do to her.

I had the arrest cars creep closer, poised to intervene if something bad began to happen. Then, to our great relief, the jogger completed her stretches and resumed her run. To this day, she most likely has no idea how close she came to what could have been the most dangerous moment of her life. Minutes later, we saw the burglars begin to load the van, filling it to the back doors with computer equipment. As they started to leave, we closed in. They tried to make a brief run for it, but within about a hundred yards, they gave up as we had them completely hemmed in. They threw their guns out the window and reached for the sky.

Here are a few practical lessons I learned about surveillance:

- Always start out with a full gas tank and some snacks. Who knows where you'll end up or when your next meal might be.
- Don't drink coffee (or anything else) before the beginning of the mission. It doesn't take long for it to reach critical mass, and you can't always duck out at will to relieve yourself. In the city, fast food joints are the best places for a quick bathroom stop. In the country, of course, the rules are much more lax.
- Try not to get the "eyeball" position where you have the primary view of the suspect you're following and have to be continuously on watch. If you're just off to the side waiting for things to start moving you can

read a book, snack on junk food, practice the harmonica—anything you might want to do to pass the time.

- If you're going to be sitting in your car for a while, shift over to the passenger's seat. Then anyone who notices you will think you're just waiting for the driver to return.

Even today I'm very familiar with most of the Twin Cities area and much of the entire state. It seemed that the crooks always knew the best routes to any destination and, by tailing them, we picked up the same knack for getting around.

13

ARMED ROBBERY

There isn't a pinch more exciting or dangerous for a cop on the street than taking down an armed robber just after the crime has happened. By its very definition, armed robbery is a violent crime that involves the use of a weapon, most often a gun. When the event takes place, the robber has reached a plateau of nervous aggression, often coupled with fear, which makes him dangerously unpredictable. When he flees the robbery scene, he's riding an adrenaline high (and often a drug-induced high) with a weapon at hand and is as close as he'll ever be to an "I won't be taken alive" mindset. Arresting someone in this state, without killing him or losing your own life, calls for a lot of skill and some luck.

I was fortunate to be at the center of two such arrests in my career. I say "fortunate" because, in the police world, a post-robbery collar ranks with grand-slam homeruns or game-winning touchdowns. It becomes part of department folklore in a world where unflinching bravery is a measure of one's worthiness.

The first situation came about when I was still a Bloomington cop working the day shift in one of the squads in the center of the city. When an "All cars" call was given out that the

Cedar Liquor Store had just been robbed, I was on the east side of my district and, on a hunch, took off on the fly for Cedar Avenue, north of the liquor store. Officer Bob Velnor and one of our detective cars were near the scene when the call came and also converged on Cedar, the main artery leading to Minneapolis. A description of the robbery car was given, and, if memory serves correctly, the detective was the first to spot the vehicle northbound on Cedar.

Many times when a robbery happened, we all guessed wrong, the crooks got away, and the case became another one for the detectives. This time, we got it just right. As the car came north on Cedar, in the area of what is now the Mall of America, Velnor and I had a moment to set up, blocking the northbound lane, and take cover behind our squads with our shotguns out. A cop's shotgun is a fearsome thing, normally loaded with four rounds of double ought buckshot, each round spraying out about a dozen lethal pea-sized pellets. I can only imagine what it must have looked like to the two robbers as they went through their options: They could try to ram their way through the two squads but would have to take multiple shotgun blasts head-on to do so; they could try to do a power turn but would be shredded by a hailstorm of lead as they spun around. From my vantage point, looking dead on through the windshield, I could see both of them deflate as they came to a stop and literally reached for the sky.

While an arrest like this was happening, I made a stream of decisions, influenced by experience and training, triggered by the suspect's actions. When it was over, I was sobered to think that I had come so close to killing someone, but, now that the handcuffs were on and everyone was intact, it was time to handle the next call. As to the possibility that I could have been the one who didn't walk away—I seldom gave it a thought.

The second robbery arrest happened after I'd left Bloomington and was a Bureau of Criminal Apprehension (BCA) agent. A Wright County investigator contacted us to say that he had informant information about a planned robbery that was to take place outside of his jurisdiction. Informants are people who, for various reasons, decide to give inside criminal information to the police. In this case, I suspect that the informant himself was well trusted in the world of crooks, probably a pretty good criminal in his own right. He had such specific knowledge of the plan that he had to have been there when it was concocted. As it was given to us, two white males, driving a white Chevy Monte Carlo with out-of-state license plates, were going to rob the Becker Liquor Store at about 11 A.M. on the following morning. The hour was a specific component of the plan, as it was, in the robbers' analysis, the most favorable time to hit the place. Both robbers were professionals and would be heavily armed.

When police learn that a violent crime is planned, they can't let it happen and then arrest the perpetrators, even though that would give them the strongest case. There is a moral obligation to protect the public. Law enforcement can't let a robber with a gun go ahead with his intentions and, perhaps, hurt someone. I thought of taking the place of the clerk and attempting to make an arrest when they came in. I would have been willing to do this, but a shootout inside the liquor store didn't seem like our best strategy. We didn't know where the robbers were staying, so we couldn't pick up surveillance on them and take them down some distance away from the store. The only real possibility seemed to be to set up on all approaches to the area, let the robbers get into the parking lot, and pounce on them as they got out of their car. The best charge we'd be able to make at that point was conspiracy to commit robbery, which only carried half the penalty of an actual robbery, but no innocent lives would be in danger.

We connected with the Sherburne County Sheriff, whose jurisdiction included Becker, and arranged for two of his men to work with five or six of our agents. Because the informant was so emphatic that the robbery was planned for 11:00, we decided to set up by 9:00. That would give us plenty of time, even if they came early. That morning we met briefly with the deputies, laid out our strategy and assignments, then headed for Becker. It happened that I was the first one out of the parking lot and got a mile or so out in front of the other agents as we traveled down Highway 10. My intention was to take up the "eyeball" position on the store itself while the other officers arranged themselves strategically to cover the area.

It was a bit before 9:00 A.M. when I cruised into the little community of Becker. The liquor store is situated right on the highway, so I could drive by, see what cars were in the lot, and then pick my vantage point. As I got within half a block of the business, I was horrified to see a white Monte Carlo parked, back end in, right in front of the entry. We should have known better than to trust a couple of robbers to follow their plan!

I barely had time to get off the highway and turn around facing the lot when I saw two men run from the liquor store and jump into the car. One of them was carrying a sack. As the suspect car rocketed onto eastbound Highway 10, I fell in behind it, meanwhile radioing the other officers who were just getting to the area. I imagine that a stickup man leaving the scene pays a lot of attention to his rearview mirror. It couldn't have been very many seconds before the robbers knew they were in trouble as a string of cars began dropping in behind them. It was mid-winter and driving was fine on the highway but, when the getaway driver turned off onto a county road, we found the surface was glare ice. On a day with nothing else to worry about, this would have been a white-knuckle drive. Traveling at high speed, heading toward a probable shootout, it was a heart-pounding situation.

About a mile down the road from Highway 10, the suspect car lost control and spun into the ditch. All of the following squads slid to rest at crazy angles. The crooks jumped out and leaped behind their car with weapons drawn, ready for a gun battle. I think, once again, it was the threat of police shotguns that made a couple of robbers rethink their strategy. Before a shot was fired, the air was filled with the sound of five or six pump shotguns being racked.

From their place behind the car, the robbers began shouting, "Don't shoot, don't shoot, we give up!" They threw out a large caliber handgun and a sawed-off rifle. It turned out they were a team of professional armed robbers from Gary, Indiana, just working their way across the country. Later, at the jail, I heard one of them, making his one phone call, tell someone, "I don't know what happened. All of a sudden, there were cops everywhere!"

Some years later, I supervised a major investigation that led to the arrests of several bigtime jewel robbers. These guys, out of the Twin Cities area, travelled the country hitting jewelry stores to the tune of many thousands of dollars in gems and watches. We also took down a local jewelry store operator who was buying some of the stolen items from the robbers and did a search warrant on the office of a sleazy defense attorney who had a hot $10,000 Rolex watch in his safe.

One of the robbers decided that it would be in his best interest to cooperate with us and testify against the other robbers. It's always interesting to get a chance to talk with someone from the other side of the fence and get his slant on the cops and robbers business. He told me about an incident that had happened to him immediately after one of his heists. He had pulled a cash robbery and was a few miles from the scene, feeling good about having gotten away. He still had the money in a bag on the front seat of his car and the gun on the floor. He was driving in traffic as he came to a red light with several cars already stopped in front of him. As he waited for the light to turn, he looked in his rearview mirror and his heart stopped. Several police cars had pulled up behind him; the cops had bailed out and were running, with drawn guns up alongside his car. "I'm busted," he thought and quickly put his hands up. The cops ran right by him to the car stopped in front of the line, where they hauled the driver out in what he took to be a drug bust. He said he shakily put his hands down and drove away when the light turned. I wondered if I had ever come that close to a good pinch and gone right on by.

14

RISKY PINCHES

There have been so many changes in the police world since I first came through the door in 1966 that it almost seems as if I lived through the transition from BC to AD. When I was young in the business, the Miranda Decision ("You have the right to remain silent...") hadn't yet been handed down; no one I worked with had heard of Mace, tasers, or extendable batons; bullet-stopping Kevlar vests or shields were still off in the future; my department-provided weaponry consisted of a Smith and Wesson .38 special Combat Master-piece revolver and a 12-gauge shotgun mounted to the dash of the squad car. Being a cop was as dangerous a proposition then as it is today; we just got by with less help and protection.

Our tactics, too, were primitive by today's standards. We took risks, sometimes crazy ones, because that's what cops did. I recall going up an outside stairway with two other officers one night to confront an angry, shotgun toting drunk who was threatening to kill people at a party. We had our .38s and no body armor; he had a 12-gauge and was holding a roomful of people at bay. If he hadn't dropped the gun when we told him to, who knows how many people might have died?

When I did my first stint in the Narcotics Division, we regularly went on drug raids. We burst into houses or apartments full of whacked-out people, weapons, and drugs, yelling "Police!!" at the top of our lungs, carried in on a tidal wave of adrenaline. Sometimes we did "buy-busts," in which an undercover agent made a drug purchase, gave a pre-arranged signal, and the covering cops swooped in to make the pinch. Imagine being in a public parking lot and suddenly seeing long-haired, shabbily dressed guys, all brandishing pistols, converging from all points of the compass on a parked vehicle. The main flaw in our strategy in those early days was that invariably some of us ended up on the driver's side, some on the passenger's side, some in front—all with our guns pointing at the drug dealer and, of course, at each other. It didn't take too many of those scenarios to make us pre-plan more. Instead of everyone competing in a footrace to the bad guy, we began to operate with specific assignments—considering lanes of fire and using some cover. It wasn't as exhilarating, but it was a much better way to operate.

One of the common characteristics within all of the cops I worked with at this time was a great thirst to be in on the action. We'd drop what we were doing and show up ready to go whenever the bell rang. We never seemed to think about how some of us might be killed. Over the years, two guys that I worked with did get shot, one fatally, the other seriously. Still, we went on, somehow believing that it couldn't happen to us.

When the signal was given to move, there was a surge of energy that propelled us forward, sometimes with unforeseen results. Once Agent John Edwards, working undercover, set up a meeting with some burglars to buy some stolen property. It was to be a buy-bust, with me and several other agents waiting as the arrest team. Edwards, driving our undercover Dodge van, met them in a restaurant parking lot. He got the crooks into the back of the van where, free from prying eyes, they could show him the merchandise. Per pre-arranged plan, Edwards would give the code word arrest signal over the body bug and we would run up to the van, open the side door, and make the arrest. It all went like clockwork, and, when the signal was given, I raced to the side of the van, grabbed the handle, and gave the door a mighty opening heave—so mighty, in fact, that the sliding door reached the end of its normal travel and kept right on going, landing with a crash beside the van. The evening ended with two thieves on their way to jail and a group of cops trying to reinstall the door on the van.

In the late 1970s, we got some first-generation Kevlar body armor at the BCA and things began to feel a bit safer. It was during that same era that we started to practice seriously for some of our most dangerous raids and arrests. We did a lot of training with SWAT Teams from Minneapolis and some of the metro area counties. In a short time, our high-risk entries went from testosterone-fueled chaos to highly disciplined, fast moving strikes. Each team member had an assignment, practiced over and over until every move was instinctive. The group would race to the entry point, usually a door, lob a flash-bang grenade through a window or the door as it was breached, and race in single file. The first guy in was the bunker man, so called because he carried a Kevlar shield, a "body bunker," in front of him. The second officer, working right over his shoulder, carried an MP-5, a compact 9mm sub-machine gun made for close-up work. They were followed by a line of SWAT guys with .40 caliber pistols. In seconds, the front team members raced to the deepest part of the house with the trailers dropping off to confront people encountered along the way. The object was to get all bad guys down on the floor before they had a chance to resist. We wanted to shock and surprise them so we wouldn't have to hurt them if they reacted violently. The unexpected thunderclap and blinding flash of the grenade was a powerful aid to this end. It took a great deal of trust among team members when we realized that other guys, weapons at the ready, would be racing in tight formation behind us, ready to shoot, we hoped, at the right target.

In 1986, I was transferred from St. Paul to the Bemidji Regional Office where I supervised BCA activities in the top half of Minnesota. Northern Minnesota is largely made up of rural counties and small towns. There were few SWAT teams in our area at that time, so that became one of our functions. We were called out to many "barricaded suspect" situations, circumstances in which an armed person (surprisingly, not always a man) was holed up in a building, often shooting from the windows at anyone who approached. The need for public safety precluded the police from just leaving the individual alone. To effect an arrest with no special training or equipment was just too risky an assignment for a handful of deputies, so they called us.

Whenever we got one of these calls, we sent out a group page to all of our team members. Agents set aside whatever else they'd been doing and converged on the scene. We did this often enough that everyone knew what to do when they got there. We'd set up a perimeter to keep the suspect in and everyone else out. Then the waiting began. We'd try to establish a way to converse with the usually troubled and angry person inside. We had several trained negotiators as part of our team, men and women who were particularly good at speaking calmly with agitated people and resolving the situation. Sometimes this worked, sometimes not.

As hours passed, if we were unable to get the person to give up peaceably, it became necessary to force a resolution. This usually involved tear gas. The theory in using gas was to flood the place, starting with the top floor and the basement, in an effort to chase the suspect to the main floor and out the door. It's not an easy decision to deploy gas because there can be mixed results. Several times, after hours of trying to negotiate the person out with no success, I directed the gas teams to go ahead. Instead of coming out, the suspect turned his gun on himself and committed suicide. Even though I recognized that this outcome may have been inevitable, it still felt bad to have given an order that was immediately followed by someone taking his own life.

The other thing about gas is that it does a lot of damage to the building. When we started gassing, we gassed the daylights out of the place. Using 37mm gas guns, we fired many liquid CS projectiles through all of the windows and, sometimes, walls. The tear gas irritant, carried by a liquid, is actually a fine powder that gets into everything, especially carpets, drapes and furniture. It usually takes professional cleaning crews with special equipment to decontaminate a place that's been gassed. It's understandably very expensive. If the place belongs to the guy who's causing the problem, no one feels bad about the aftermath. Sometimes, though, the building owner has no part in the situation; then who's responsible—morally, ethically, financially, and legally?

Our group worked with some other teams in South St. Paul in a situation in which an armed burglar fled randomly into a house from which he held the pursuing officers at bay. After hours of fruitlessly talking to him through a bullhorn, we gassed the place very thoroughly. When he still didn't come out, a team of officers had to go in after him. They found him in the attic where he had minimized the effects of the gas by crawling under some bats of insulation. After they had pulled him down and cuffed him, he got to feel the full effects of the tear gas. Who could blame the SWAT guys, who had gas masks, if they walked slowly as they took him down the stairs and out of the house? In the aftermath, I heard that the City of South St. Paul ended up buying the house.

It's one thing to wait patiently and let a situation play out when the troops are able to set up and maintain a tight perimeter around the trouble site; it can be quite another thing in the harsh winter environment in the northern reaches of our state. One night we had a call for help in Roseau County, located just south of the Canadian border. When deputies tried to approach a man in a farmhouse, he fired on them, narrowly missing them and probably causing them to rethink their career choices. When we got our team together, it was dark and the mercury was at -37 degrees. I had no thought of setting up perimeters or patiently negotiating.

Let's just go in and gas him out. A group of agents waded along a fence line through knee-deep snow to the rear of the house. We borrowed a big dump truck from the county. With the dump box raised as a bullet-deflecting shield, the sheriff backed up the driveway, SWAT members jogging behind, using the truck as cover. In the fifteen minutes or so that it took to get into position, I'm sure that our liquid CS had frozen solid. We immediately began firing tear gas popsicles through the upper windows, and moments later the man ran out with his hands up.

As a couple of the agents put him on the ground and were handcuffing him, the man said, "Am I crazy?"

"Yes, you are," one of the agents replied, "but we're going to get you some help."

An even higher pressure problem is when an armed suspect takes hostages. I was the team commander for three of these situations. The first happened just after I transferred to Bemidji. A teenage student at Park Rapids High School brought a pistol to school and took one of the teachers hostage. One of our negotiators was able to talk to the boy on a telephone in the classroom and eventually convinced him to put down his weapon and surrender. While this was going on, I was in the hallway right around the corner from the classroom, thinking about how much I did not want to shoot a high school kid. I was almost as glad as the teacher when he gave up.

The second hostage situation happened in Little Falls, a small town about 120 miles south of Bemidji. We got a call early in the morning that a man had entered an apartment where his ex-wife was staying and was threatening to kill her. Even with lights and sirens, it takes a while to get to a scene that far away. By the time we got part of our group there, things had deteriorated badly; the people talking to the hostage-taker on the phone believed that he had already done something to his ex-wife. We put a rescue team together on the fly, crashed into the apartment, disarmed the man, and began giving first aid to the young woman who, we found, had been stabbed. She had already lost a great deal of blood and, in spite of our best efforts, died on the way to the hospital. Even though it's unreasonable, there's always a sense of failure with such an outcome.

The third situation was in Cass County. A man was holding several people in a rural farm house. We had a twelve-hour standoff during which the prospects for peaceful resolution seemed to come and go. While the hostage-taker was distracted, several of the hostages escaped, leaving one young woman still in his control. At one point the negotiator told me he felt the man was getting ready to kill the woman. Stationed in the woods near the house, we had several snipers who caught occasional glimpses of the man through the windows. I told them if they got a clean shot at the man to take it. A short time later the tide in the negotiation took a turn for the better, and I rescinded the shoot order. Eventually the man released the woman and surrendered. When he came out, contrary to the instructions he'd received, the suspect was still carrying a gun. As the man cleared the building, Agent Steve Hagenah, who was concealed nearby, called out to him to drop the gun. By Hagenah's description, the man froze, seemed to think about it for a few moments, then dropped the gun and gave up. So narrow is the space between life and death in these events.

Reminiscing about thirty-seven years of armed confrontations and other high-risk situations, I sometimes wonder how close I might have come to having my name inscribed on the National Police Memorial Monument. I'll never know the answer. The event that gave me the greatest pause, after the fact, was one in which a barricaded suspect shot several rounds through a wall when I was firing tear gas into the house. When the confrontation was over, I looked at the bullet holes and the spot where I had been standing.

How did he miss me? I asked myself.

The Outlaws arrested. Officers Smith and Glynn guard three suspects.

The author receives a commendation for saving the life of a heart attack victim. Pictured are Glenn Kuschel, Chief Clarence Coster, Smith, Captain Henry Schrader, and Lt. Charles Anderson. Photo by Irv Norling

Terry Smith in uniform

NARC NEWS

NARC INFORMATION BULLETIN*********

Dear Hundred Flowers

I would like to give you some information that may save my boothers and sisters from the grief I had to go through. I was busted by two narcotic agents on the 15th (1) a Dennis Sigafoos 5'6"-5'7", dark brown almost black hair with a mustache and the early start of a beard. He occasionally dyes his hair. (2) a Terry Smith 5'11" thick black hair, long sideburns. They are known to wear green army coats. Dennis Sigafoos used to be a member of the Edina Police Dept He drives a bright red mustange. Terry Smith drives a light blue mustange. Donie Durst a member of Edina High School was the informer. I hope within the next few weeks or perhaps before I will have all of their pictures. We have got to get together and stop these people. Bring them out in the open so everyone will know who the bad guys are before it's too late. The games they play aren't fun.

Your Sister

"Narc News," printed in "Hundred Flowers," a
counterculture newspaper.

BCA Organized Crime Unit in gangster mode. Picture by Roger Pappke

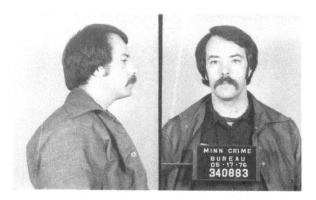

BCA undercover agent Terry Smith

MISSING — 7/29/98

JULIE ANN HOLMQUIST
AGE 16
HALLOCK, MN

HEIGHT: 5'6"
WEIGHT: 150 LBS,
EYES:BLUE
HAIR: BLONDE

LAST SEEN WEARINC DARK-COLORED SHORTS RED OR WHITE TOP, AN]: DARK-COLORED ROLLFF BLADES.

IF SEEN, PLEASE CONTACT:

**KITTSON CO.
SHERIFF'S OFFICE
218-843-3535**

**TOLL-FREE
TIP LINE
1-888-843-2125**

Missing person poster, Julie Holmquist

POSSIBLE KIDNAPPING / STRANGER ABDUCTION

Kathlyn Elizabeth Poirier (Katie)   DOB/022880

5' 4" tall, 115 lbs., brunette hair, wearing light wgt slacks and a light colored top

If you have any information, please contact the Carlton County Sheriff's Department at (218-384-9135 or 1-888-424-1935).

Missing person poster, Katie Poirier

15

BOOKIES

From 1975 until sometime in the early 1980s, I was assigned to the BCA's Organized Crime Unit. It could more accurately have been named the Major Crime Unit, since Minnesota didn't have in residence the kind of heavy-duty Mafia families found in some other parts of the country. We did have sophisticated criminal enterprises, though, with sinister overtones of political corruption and shadowy connections between bad guys and those who were supposed to be on our side. It was an exciting assignment; the unit had an "Elliot Ness" sort of feel as we went after criminals who had been too successful for too long. Our job description, in the most realistic terms, was "Catch Big Crooks." Idealism and enthusiasm carried us along to a number of notable successes. There were also a few times when we found that the forces of unrighteousness, with the help of well-placed friends, could unravel our best efforts.

Most of the time we pursued people who were active in traditional criminal enterprise: chop shop owners, stolen property fences, robbery/burglary groups, outlaw biker gangs. Sometimes in the fall, if we had nothing else pressing, we busted bookies.

Sports betting in the United States is a colossal business.

According to the website *legalsportsbetting.com*, $5.32 billion
worth of sports bets was placed in Las Vegas in 2019. The same
website estimates that about $150 billion was bet nationally that
year. Some people are so addicted to gambling that they'll bet on
anything throughout the year, but the fall football season seemed
to draw the greatest activity. We had good intelligence on many
of the major bookies; the nature of the business made them creatures of habit, so they were easy targets for surveillance. A group
of Jewish bookies, for instance, would regularly meet at the
Lincoln Dell Restaurant in St. Louis Park. It was simple to see
who was there and perhaps overhear some of their discussions.
Often, we were able to come up with informants who could place
bets with certain bookies. Combining that information with what
we already knew, it became a matter of choosing the right time
and place to move in while the betting action was at its peak.

A bookmaker is not a gambler. He is, rather, a businessman
who takes bets, some that will win, some that will lose, from
people who are into gambling. His profit, called "vigorish," is a
kind of surtax paid by the losers. Here's how it works: Early in
the week the bookie contacts his connection from whom he gets
"the line," the point spread for games coming up that week. The
point spread is a handicapper's attempt to make both sides of
each contest equally attractive to bet on. Let's say the Vikings,
who are having a great season, are playing the Lions, who have
an injured quarterback and have lost their past four games. The
line might be Vikings -8 (or Lions +8). When the game's over,
you'll subtract eight points from the Vikings score to determine
which side won the bet. By midweek, bettors are contacting the
bookie for the line and beginning to place bets, which they may
do right up until the kickoff. There's always a big flurry of
betting just before each contest. After the weekend action is over,
the bookmaker settles up with his bettors, giving the amount bet
to the winners and collecting the bet plus 10% vigorish from the
losers. If you bet $100 on a game and your team beat the spread,

you'd receive that amount; if you lost, you'd pay $110. The bookie's goal is to get about the same amount of money bet on both sides of each event. He has several tricks to help accomplish that. If he's successful, his take for the weekend is 5% of his "handle," or total volume of bets. If his handle was $50,000 in bets and he was able to balance them equally, his profit would be $2500.

The first bookmaking investigation that I did was in Duluth in the mid-1970s. We'd been told by Duluth PD detectives that they'd heard rumors of heavy betting action taking place at two adjacent locations on Superior Street—the Paul Bunyan Bar and the Silver Hammer Bar. There had been no previous enforcement efforts, so things were pretty wide open.

We began running surveillance, putting undercover agents on the inside and watching people come and go from the outside. It didn't take long to figure out that there was betting going on in both places. Al Nisius, the manager at the Paul Bunyan, had a steady stream of people coming to see him. During conversations with them and during frequent phone calls received by him, he made notations in an ever-present spiral notebook. Some cash exchanges were observed and some betting discussions, overheard.

It appeared that a bartender at the Silver Hammer was taking bets and forwarding them to someone else. We saw the same kind of interaction with customers, but he would just make notations on slips of paper. A few minutes before kick-off time, the bartender would go to a payphone in the entryway and place a call, referring to the slips as he talked. Having seen this, we timed it so that an undercover agent passed through just as the bartender got on the phone. He was able to overhear some betting-type conversation.

After a few weeks of sporadic surveillance, we had enough information to get search warrants for both bars. Because they were open to the public, there were no raids to plan or special efforts to make to keep the operators from destroying their records; we just walked in, search warrants in hand. It was most interesting to get a look at Nisius' spiral notebook. It had records for all of the action he'd handled that fall, totaling, as I recall, about $1.5 million in bets. One of the officers who took him to jail reported that Nisius was most indignant when he noted the name of the judge who had signed the search warrant. We came to understand that better during a future investigation.

Impressed as I was by Nisius' betting business, I found that he was small time compared to some of the bookmakers in the Minneapolis/St. Paul area. In time, we raided a number of them, and it was surprising to see the volume of bets that flowed through their operations.

As we increased our enforcement efforts it became a real cat-and-mouse situation between cops and bookies. To make our case we had to develop "probable cause," the legal term for information specific and persuasive enough to convince a judge to issue a search warrant for the place where the bookie would be doing business. The warrant had to be executed at a time when gambling records were present and, preferably, when bets were coming in by telephone. We had to get in quickly enough to prevent anyone from destroying the vital papers.

The bookmakers, for their part, were forced to do certain things that made them more vulnerable. There were no cell phones in those days, so they used old-fashioned landline telephones to receive bets. The timing of the calls was predictable because there was always concentrated activity just before the weekend games and on Monday evenings. While some betting customers were reliable enough just to keep a tab running, there were always some bettors to meet and settle up with in person each week.

A raid on an illegal betting operation had to be tightly chore-ographed and rapidly executed to be successful. We would always have a "no-knock" search warrant, authorizing us to do whatever was necessary to get in quickly. We'd approach as covertly as possible, then rush up to the door and blast it open with a sledge hammer, yelling, "Police! Search warrant!" at the top of our voices. We shouted "Police!" for two reasons: because the courts wanted us to and because a suspect in Minneapolis had been found not guilty of shooting two plainclothes officers as they executed a search warrant on his place. He claimed he didn't know they were cops and thought he was protecting himself from burglars. If we took a bullet, we at least wanted someone to go to jail for it. Usually, the shock of the entrance would delay the reaction of those inside long enough to let us get to the records before they could destroy them.

Each case we made was a learning opportunity both for the cops and the bookmakers. While we learned about how they conducted their operations, they learned ways to make it more difficult for us to catch them in the act. Some began using call forwarding and changing locations frequently. Some ran a telephone line from the apartment listed for the telephone to another apartment, perhaps upstairs. When they heard the door coming down in apartment A, they would begin destroying records and shutting down the operation in apartment B. Eventually water-soluble paper became the industry standard for recording bets. When we entered, it was a footrace to get to the records before they could be plunged into a waiting bucket of water. Agent Joy Rikala, one of my partners in many gambling investigations, began carrying a hair dryer as standard raid equipment. If we could grab a clump of paper before it completely dissolved, she could often salvage usable evidence.

In many parts of the country, gambling was controlled by organized crime. In Minnesota, as far as we could tell, sports bookmaking was done by freelancers who knew and, sometimes, cooperated with each other, but acted independently.

I did hear a chilling story about one aborted attempt to change that. We arrested a professional armed robber for a series of jewelry heists. We had such solid and serious charges against him that he decided to cooperate with us. He told me that at one time he and another very violent robber had been contacted by a well-known Minneapolis crime figure with a plan to take control of bookmaking in Minneapolis and St. Paul. Our informant and his partner were to kidnap and brutally murder one of the Jewish bookies. The word would then be spread to the rest of the book-makers that they could be next unless they started paying tribute to the would-be kingpin. The two robbers started out one evening to carry out the plan. They went to a pizza place owned by the intended victim and found that they had just missed him. For the rest of the evening, they went from place to place, never catching up with him. Late that evening, the two robbers had a severe falling out and forgot about the murder plan.

There was never the kind of animosity between us and the bookies that we often felt with other people we had arrested. For one thing, they seemed to regard being busted as just an occupa-tional hazard. Probably the big reason, though, was that book-making at that time in Minnesota was just a gross-misdemeanor carrying a maximum $1,000 fine. They could peel that from their roll of cash, toss it on the clerk-of-court's desk, and be back in business within a few days, not feeling much pain at all. The money was just too good, all of it tax-free, for them even to consider changing occupations.

At the beginning of one National Football League season, I had a great brainstorm that ended up causing us no end of aggra-vation and disgust. A year or so earlier, we'd gone back to Duluth and again busted Al Nisius and another bookie with the usual results.

Maybe, I reasoned, *if we made cases on all of the major bookies in Duluth and also charged any people we could identify as having placed bets with them, it would have a real impact on a pretty serious vice problem in the city.*

"Good idea," was the response from cops and prosecutors

when I presented the idea. In December, we hit it hard, gathering a wealth of evidence on five bookmakers and many bettors. Because there was so much information to put together, it took some period of time to get everything in order. The volume of trial work that could ensue caused the county attorney to ask for help from the Minnesota Attorney General's Office. A young lawyer whom we liked and respected was assigned. So far, so good.

The first inkling of trouble came in the late spring when I got a call from the city attorney who would be prosecuting the bettors. He told me that some of the people on our list to be charged were very wealthy or influential; three of them were lawyers, one of them was a former judge.

That's great, I thought. *People like that should be held to a higher standard of behavior than the garbage men and plumbers that no one seems to be concerned about.* How naïve I was.

When a person was to be charged with committing a crime, a legal complaint was drafted, listing the particulars of the crime. The complaint was then signed by a judge, the defendant was notified of the charges, and the system moved along to an eventual conclusion. In early summer, the complaints against all of the bettors were presented to a judge. He refused to sign the ones against the three attorneys. In the following days they were passed from judge to judge with all judges refusing to sign them.

During this process our lawyer from the Attorney General's Office told us he'd had a face-to-face conversation with one of the attorney/gamblers. The man said that he was a close personal friend of the Minnesota Attorney General and planned to have dinner with him that evening.

"If you ever want to go anywhere with your career, you'd better drop the charges against me," he said. Later that evening our lawyer was contacted by his supervisor in St. Paul who told him they were pulling him off of the gambling prosecutions.

On the following day, Duluth Police Department Lieutenant

Gary Waller and I went to see one of the judges. We asked him what the remedy was when all of the judges refused to sign the complaints. The judge replied that it wasn't his problem and he wouldn't do anything to help us. He said that people like these attorneys shouldn't be charged with placing bets and he'd do everything in his power to stop us. He succeeded. The three were never charged.

When I got back to St. Paul, one of my BCA superiors called me into his office. "Do you know what the trouble with you is?" he said. "You see everything in black and white. You need to realize that there are a lot of shades of gray in some situations."

I'm still that way. To me, doing things that are against the law is clearly wrong. A penalty that applies to one with no power or influence should also apply to the Attorney General's friend. In my world, cops, judges, and lawyers should be the last ones to receive a "get out of jail free card." A system that plays favorites is, in my view, corrupt and morally reprehensible.

Sometime in the 1990s, I had one more go around with Al Nisius. Knowing of my past interest in Al, one of the Duluth cops invited me to go along on a raid on his current operation in a rundown apartment above a business in downtown Duluth. When we hit the place, the phones were ringing off the hook with people calling in bets. During the search we found $10,000 in cash hidden in a closet. We also found a safe deposit key from a downtown bank. A search warrant there netted another $100,000. This time instead of just peeling $1,000 from his bankroll, he got to discuss the entire matter with the Internal Revenue Service. I'd have been willing to wager that he wouldn't see much of his money again, but he would have been too disgruntled to take my bet.

16

CHASE ON THE LAKE

I t was an early winter morning. There had been a few weeks of pretty cold weather, but the temps had moderated and a freezing rain had fallen during the night. The side roads were treacherous as I started for the Bemidji BCA Office. It was a relief to get out to Highway 71, a main thoroughfare, and find that sand and salt, courtesy of the Minnesota Department of Transportation, had turned the icy sheen into a messier but safer surface.

As on every day that I was in my BCA squad, the police radio was scanning all of the local channels: Bemidji PD, Beltrami and Cass Counties, State Patrol, and others. We interacted with the local cops all the time, working investigations together, rolling to a scene if someone called for help, keeping an eye out for a vehicle or suspect that we knew they were looking for. I had just passed the Highway 2 bypass when Beltrami County put out a call on a theft that had just occurred at the Cenex Station, giving license number and description of a car in which the thieves had fled.

I just drove by there, I thought, and pulled over to the side of the road to see if the car came by northbound. Moments later, I heard one of our agents, Dan Ahlquist, on the Beltrami channel saying, "I've got that theft car going south on Highway 71." I turned south and stomped on it, thinking that I'd help Ahlquist track the car until we could vector the local cops into position to stop it, whereupon we'd go on with our previously intended business. Most cops are adrenaline junkies, always wanting in on whatever action is taking place. This sort of thing was especially delightful for the BCA folks, because we could join in, get our little burst of excitement, and then go on without having to write reports or haul anyone to jail.

At first, the suspects probably didn't know they were in trouble because Ahlquist's unmarked car wouldn't have raised any concern. I caught up with them at about County Road 9, a few miles to the south, just as a Beltrami squad and a State Patrol car joined the procession. Under normal circumstances, Ahlquist and I would have hung around just long enough to see that the car stop went OK, then left. Everything changed when the Beltrami dispatcher said, "Cars on the theft call, be advised we had a gun call involving that car earlier." Now we were in full backup mode.

The suspect car turned east onto County Road 9, and it became clear that they didn't intend to stop for the flashing red lights behind them. The chase, on glare ice, was on. A police chase is like a snowball travelling downhill. As it rolls along, it continues to pick up squad cars along the way. We sailed along, at crazy speed for the conditions. By the time we reached Highway 371, about twelve miles down the road, we'd picked up another State Patrol unit and several more county squads.

There's been a longstanding national debate about good guy/bad guy vehicular pursuits. Every time an innocent third party is hurt by a fleeing suspect, some people proclaim that all police chases should be banned. The other side then responds, "You mean by simply stepping on the accelerator anyone should be able to issue himself a 'Get out of jail free card'?" Most departments do have policies that regulate these situations, and no police officer wants to endanger anyone unnecessarily, so the cops are always under a lot of pressure to be as circumspect as possible while attempting to catch the suspect. The "chasees," on the other hand, seem to segue into a death defying, nothing-else-matters state that endangers everyone who might get in the way.

The bad guys hurtled across 371, a busy state highway, without slowing down. The cop cars all slowed long enough to see that the way was clear, then followed. During the next five minutes we toured some back roads, returned to 371, paraded down the main street of the small town of Cass Lake, and crossed Highway 2, all with red lights flashing and six or eight sirens blaring. I imagine it was more entertainment than the local folks had seen in some time.

It was after we'd crossed Highway 2 that it looked as if the chase was going to come to an end. The suspect car took a right turn onto a secondary road, and one of the deputies radioed, "We should have them now; this dead ends at the lake." Imagine our surprise, moments later, when the car we thought we were going to bottle up at the end of the road simply hurtled through the snow bank and continued out onto the frozen lake.

Now I must explain two things to make the rest of this narrative make sense:

First, the frozen lake. Those of you who live in warmer climates will have to take my word for this: Where I live, we drive on frozen lakes all winter. Some students at Bemidji State University even take advantage of unlimited free parking on the lake in front of the college when the ice gets thick enough. "Thick enough," though, is the key phrase. It takes a minimum of about twelve inches of good ice to support a full-sized vehicle safely. (I like two feet.) Every year after the lakes freeze over, fishermen are anxious to get out and drill some holes. They'll start by walking onto the lake. A few days or weeks later, when the ice is thicker, they'll use an all-terrain vehicle or snowmobile. Finally, after we've had some good cold weather and a lot of holes have been drilled, some people will begin to drive their trucks out. If they don't go through the ice, pretty soon everyone is doing it.

Second, the psychology of a police chase. When a car runs from us, it seems as if they ought not get away with that. As the chase proceeds, we become more and more focused on catching them, almost no matter what. We are all careful enough of the welfare of others that we would never blow through an intersection without slowing and checking for traffic, but our tolerance for our own personal risk goes up and up. Adrenaline begins to flow in great amounts, and we get madder and madder at the suspects and their reckless disregard for anybody who might get in the way. Big departments that have a lot of pursuit situations will usually have a supervisor who is not involved in the chase but is monitoring on the radio. That supervisor will weigh everything that is happening, consider public safety, and decide whether to allow the chase to continue or to call it off. What might be a difficult decision for an uninvolved supervisor is nearly an impossible one for a cop in hot pursuit.

Here's the thing: This was early enough in the winter that no one had yet determined whether the ice was thick enough to drive on. Was it four inches thick? Eight inches? A foot? None of us knew. But the suspect car was moving along just fine, so naturally we all just sailed onto the lake after it. It would have been interesting to look down on our formation from above. Everyone was concerned about our collective weight and we all spread out in a big "V" formation. One of the trooper cars moved up behind the car we were chasing and radioed that he was going to "pit" the car, meaning to give it a glancing blow with his bumper and throw it into a spin. We all fell back, the trooper gave it a bump, and both cars disappeared into a huge volcano of snow. Suddenly the patrol car shot out from one side of the cloud. The suspect car flew out the other side, corrected its course, and continued on.

Then something happened that I had never seen before: The front window on the passenger's side rolled down, and a man climbed out and sat on the window sill with only his legs inside the car. He began to throw beer cans at the nearest squad, apparently attempting to take out its windshield. Someone inside the car must have been handing the cans to him, because he had thrown about a twelve-pack's worth before he climbed back into the car. Either he'd gotten cold or, more likely, run out of ammunition. After he was safely back inside the car, a county squad moved up and gave the car a glancing blow that put it out of commission and ended the chase. As we all jumped out of our cars and ordered the suspects out of theirs, the character who had been throwing the beer cans jumped out, dropped into a crouch position, and began pretend-shooting at us with his hand. It was fortunate for him that everyone could clearly see that he didn't actually have a weapon.

I covered the driver's side of the car and was surprised to see a young woman, probably eighteen or twenty, get out from behind the wheel. I put her down on the ice and was guarding her there when I heard an anguished voice say, "Roxanne!"

It was one of the local officers who had heard the chase and found that his worst fears had been realized. His daughter had been the driver. As he knelt by her on the ice, he turned to me and said, "She's been running with these guys for the past three weeks. I tried to stop her, but I couldn't." Suddenly I saw her not just as a suspect handcuffed on the ice, but also as a prodigal daughter who had broken her father's heart.

With the chase over and all four of the suspects in custody, we couldn't get off the lake quickly enough. Without the help of adrenaline, our devil-may-care attitudes melted away, and it felt wonderful to get back to the shore. I'm sure every cop involved would now agree that the only sensible thing would have been to stop at the end of the road. Like so many things that happened when I was on the job, because it all turned out OK, I wouldn't have missed it for anything. My only regret: None of the squads had a dash-mounted video camera.

17

CON MEN

During my time as a cop, I met a lot of people who lied. Some were fairly adept at it; many were not. From time to time, I encountered someone who used dishonesty as a tool and did it with such finesse that it was difficult not to believe him even when you thought he might be lying. As in the movie "The Sting," deft lies and seemingly corroborating circumstances can push even a skeptic into buying a phony scenario.

When I was in the Organized Crime Unit, we heard from a suburban Twin Cities detective that he was working a case in which a group of employees at a manufacturing plant had put up money to buy a number of television sets at a greatly discounted price. The cash had been collected by a fellow worker who gave it to the person selling the TV sets, expecting immediate delivery and high-fives all around. Like an illusionist, the guy who'd been handed the envelope of currency did a vanishing act, leaving the buyer with no cash and no television sets. He had a lot of explaining to do to his fellow workers. No one could be sure if the man who collected the money had made the whole thing up and stolen the cash himself or if they all had been royally fleeced. *What a bunch of dopes!* was our immediate reaction.

A few weeks later we heard a similar story from another source. Was it the same situation, simply reported by another person who'd been defrauded? Delving into the details, we found that we were hearing about two different but very similar events. This was getting more interesting!

I regularly attended monthly investigators' meetings in both Ramsey and Hennepin Counties, the two big governing entities that took in most of the metro area at that time. Detectives from many suburban departments as well as Minneapolis and St. Paul got together to share information that could be of mutual interest. Having heard the fraudulent TV story twice now, I inquired if anyone had similar cases. I was surprised to learn of several other identical thefts or attempted thefts scattered around the Twin Cities area. It appeared that some person or group had a pretty good racket going.

In each case, the approach had been the same: A fast-talking male caller, identifying himself as "Joe from Consolidated Freightways," phoned the head shipping clerk in a large business. The caller knew the clerk's first name and acted as if they'd met before. The clerk, who interacted with a lot of people, couldn't quite place "Joe," but felt as if he might know him. "Joe" said that Consolidated Freightways had a problem he was trying to resolve: Through a clerical error they had somehow ended up with an over-shipment of Motorola TV sets, more than their normal outlet could handle. It would cost his company more to ship them back to the point of manufacture than it would to let them go quickly at a steep discount. The caller's boss had instructed him to sell them off at one-fourth retail value, $100 for portable sets, $200 for consoles. "Joe" wondered if there would be people in the clerk's workplace who'd be interested in a good deal on a TV set. It would be a strictly cash transaction; all sales would be final. He couldn't guarantee they'd be available for long because he would be calling a number of his other customers and thought that they'd go fairly quickly. "Joe" didn't leave a call back number, saying that he'd be tied up making calls or delivering TVs, but he would phone the next day to see if the clerk had any takers.

Most people hearing a sales pitch like this would be skeptical. Later, when we interviewed some of the victims, we found that at first they thought the proposition sounded fishy. They admitted to believing the TV sets might be stolen property or that "Joe" might be pulling a fast one on his company. Whatever doubt or guilt they felt over that possibility was quickly tamped down by the temptation of getting a tremendous deal on a really nice TV set. If the sets were "hot," they had no knowledge of that and, therefore, no culpability. They rationalized that they would be doing business with Consolidated Freightways, a reputable shipping company with which they were familiar. The shipping clerk had the impression that "Joe" was someone with whom he'd done business before. There was also some pressure to act quickly: Employees in other companies were being offered the same great deal. Think this over too carefully and the whole deal might evaporate! One possibility that didn't seem to occur to anybody was that there might not be any television sets at all.

In each workplace where the word spread that a fellow employee could get a fabulous deal on brand new expensive TVs, co-workers lined up with money in their hands. Within hours there were many people saying, "Get me one," (or two or three) and forking over the cash. When "Joe" called back, he must have been pleased to hear the numbers quoted by the shipping clerk. Arrangements were made for the transaction in a location near a warehouse or freight yard. The employee with the cash met with "Joe" and then, inexplicably, with no TVs in sight, handed over the cash, whereupon "Joe" disappeared, never to be heard from again.

"How could anybody be that stupid?" is the question that

sprang to the lips of everyone who heard about the one-way transaction. The people who handed over the cash asked themselves the same thing—after the fact. One of the victims gave us a blow-by-blow description of the way in which he was fleeced of about $2000. When "Joe" called back, the clerk told him he had money to buy a number of TVs. "Joe" said the merchandise would be transferred at the loading dock at the big Wards Midway store on University Avenue in St. Paul. They set a time to meet; the buyer was to bring a U-Haul truck to haul the sets, and "Joe" would meet him there. The victim said that, as he was driving to the meet location, he reminded himself over and over that he had to inspect the goods before paying the money. When he pulled into the loading dock area, at first he saw no one. Then, suddenly, a man was at his truck window, shaking his hand, introducing himself as the man with the TVs.

The victim described the seller as very friendly and fast talking, having what sounded like a New York accent. He said, "Come on, we'll get your TVs for you," and led him onto the loading dock. There were two Wards warehouse employees sitting on the edge of the dock eating sandwiches.

"Having lunch, boys?" the TV man asked.

"Yeah," they replied.

When they had moved out of earshot of the two, the TV man said, "I have to watch those two all the time or I'd never get any work out of them."

They came to a set of warehouse doors marked "Employees Only" where the salesman said, "Your sets are here in the warehouse. I'll take the money to Anne in accounting and get a receipt for you. If you back up to the loading dock, I'll have those two bozos cut their lunch break short and load them up for you."

The bamboozled buyer handed his envelope of cash to the salesman, who walked through the warehouse doors and out of sight. With a sinking feeling, after waiting by his truck for several minutes, the buyer asked the warehouse employees what might be keeping their boss. They said, "We've never seen that guy before." It seemed that "Joe," or whoever he was, had simply walked through the warehouse and out another door.

"It all just went really fast," the victim said.

After pulling together what details we could get about these thefts, I talked to the head of security at Consolidated Freightways. He told me this sort of scam was being pulled in cities all across the country by a group of people who seemed to operate from a common script. Even though his company was not involved in any way, the situation was causing problems for Consolidated Freightways because of the use of the company name.

We put an intelligence bulletin out to all metro area police departments, advising them of the scam and asking them to call us if they heard of anyone who'd been contacted by the con men. Our hope was that we could catch the thieves in the act. Within a few days, we got the lucky break we'd been waiting for. A detective from the Bloomington Police Department (my alma mater) called to say he'd just received a report from a shipping clerk at an engineering company that a caller had offered to sell a shipment of TV sets at an unusually low price. The clerk had played along with the caller and volunteered to cooperate with the police. He was currently waiting for a call back from the TV salesman. I raced to meet with Bloomington detectives and the shipping clerk. We instructed him to pretend to be ready to purchase a number of sets and get instructions for a time and place to meet. When the call was received, he was told to get a truck and meet "Joe" at a fast-food restaurant in Bloomington. He would be led from there to the merchandise.

We wired the clerk with a body bug and mounted a foot and vehicle surveillance of the meeting site. He drove to the location and parked. As we watched, a rental car with three male occupants cruised through the lot near the truck, then pulled to the opposite side of the parking lot. One man got out and walked to the truck while the other two watched from a distance. We listened on the bug while the TV salesman began his routine. When the transaction had gone as far as it could without the clerk handing over an envelope of cash, we swooped in and arrested con man #1. When this happened, his accomplices saw the action and tried to race out of the lot but were cut off and arrested by Bloomington officers.

Through diligent follow-up investigation during the rest of that day and evening, we identified a second three-man team of con men who were staying at the same Bloomington hotel where the in-custody trio had been registered. By about 2:00 A.M., we had developed enough probable cause to pound on their hotel room doors and notify them that they were under arrest for theft.

They were an interesting group of people. All six had flown in from New York City and had extensive criminal records for crimes involving theft, fraud, gambling, and drugs. Several had active arrest warrants. It seemed that, with each group, there was one older, fast talking man who was the set-up caller. A second man, a bit younger was the person who met the victims. The third, younger still, was just a helper who drove the car and picked up the money man after the theft.

In the possession of one of the older men, we seized a spiral notebook listing many major cities across the country. Under the heading of each city was very detailed information on many restaurants and businesses that appeared to be places to meet intended victims. There also were listings of manufacturing plants and large businesses, complete with phone numbers, apparently of suggested victims. It appeared that someone had done a great deal of work putting the scheme together.

With the publicity that this case received, we were able to find out about four successful TV fraud thefts in the Minneapolis/St. Paul area ranging from $1,500 to $4,200. We also received word of a number of attempted set-ups in which the intended victims didn't fall for the routine.

The six deceptive wise-guys from the east were all charged with appropriate theft-related crimes. I wasn't called to testify in any trials for any of them and moved on to other things. I imagine they all did some plea bargaining, took the best sentencing deal available, and shook the dust of the Twin Cities from their feet as they left town.

Today I doubt that anyone would work as hard or put themselves in as much jeopardy as these imaginary TV salesmen did for a fairly modest return on their efforts. There are still people around who enjoy fleecing others and feel no remorse in doing so. Now they do it on the internet or through the phone or in fraudulent credit transactions and reap profits that would boggle the minds of those old con men. Unless, of course, it's the same guys and they've now become high-tech!

18

PITBULL PANDEMONIUM

Most of the police raids that I led were the culmination of an investigation in which I'd been involved. Once in a while I was asked to plan an arrest scenario for a case that had not been mine. Perhaps my peers had been impressed by some past successes, or, more likely, they wanted someone else to do the planning and bear the responsibility for a risky venture that may or may not turn out well. In the spring of 1981, Agents Mike Cummings and Paul Gerber came to me for help with the conclusion of a case they'd been working on involving gambling on pit bull fights.

When Gerber and Cummings first mentioned that they were investigating dog fighting, I was unimpressed. I had an image of the old mixed-breed dog I had when I was a kid tangling in a territorial dispute with one of his rivals in the neighborhood. When they explained that they were looking at highly organized activity involving gambling, using specially trained dogs, and operating covertly, it sounded like a bigger deal.

The case had been put together well, using an informant who was able to bring one of our female agents, posing as his girl-friend, to a meeting with several key members of the dog fighting group. She heard details of an upcoming fight to be held at a rural property about forty miles north of the Twin Cities. It was to be an important event with dogs and people coming from several other mid-western states. The investigators wanted to hit the place when things were in full swing. To accomplish that feat meant getting an arrest force to a secluded area without alerting the dogfighters, controlling a crowd of about fifty or more possibly unruly people, and handling a number of dogs bred for their savagery. It sounded like a tactical problem I could get my teeth into.

Any time we planned a rural raid, we tried to assemble whatever information we could get on the lay of the land, the arrangement of buildings, and the features of the surrounding area. I got a State Patrol pilot to do an over flight and take pictures of the property. In studying the photos, I was initially puzzled by what looked like a number of small crop circles in a field behind the buildings. Upon closer inspection, I realized that they had been worn by chains attaching dogs to stakes at the centers of the circles. The surrounding area was wooded and swampy. When we went in, we'd have to watch out for the dogs and try to keep members of the crowd bottled up so they couldn't escape into the woods.

To this point the inquiry had not been a manpower burner. Cummings and Gerber had done most of the prep work with only occasional help from others. As I thought about the raid, it seemed obvious that, for the safety of good guys and bad guys, it would be necessary to use a significant number of cops to hit the event. I wanted to go in with enough force that people wouldn't even think of resisting. I'd be able to draw troops from the State Patrol, Chisago and Washington County Sheriffs' Departments, Forest Lake Police Department, and my own agency. Plenty of enforcement help should be available. Dealing with people was something we would be able to handle; dealing with fighting dogs was not at all in our area of expertise. For this I planned to draw on the Minnesota Humane Society.

The dog fight event was planned for late evening, so we would have the advantage of darkness to get our forces close to the target location. I just had to think of an efficient way to get about sixty officers into the area and quickly and strategically deployed when it was time to strike. Darkness would also be a disadvantage, making it difficult for our forces to move on foot into unfamiliar territory or see running fight attendees who may make a break for it. To counter this last problem, I lined up a State Patrol helicopter to swoop in on my command and illuminate the scene with a monstrous floodlight mounted under the aircraft.

Using our secure radio system, I would choreograph the entire effort, directing the various elements as their turns came to act. My first thought was to do this from the helicopter. I envisioned being up in a spot where I could move the elements around like chessmen and watch things unfold from on high. I decided to stay on the ground because I guessed that, with all of the action occurring after dark, there might not be any advantage with an aerial viewpoint. As things played out, it was a fortunate decision for me.

Word came from our informant that the dogfight was now definitely on for the late evening of May 2. It would be at the previously identified home of Edward Booth, the event's organizer. The game was afoot.

Several things concerned me as we approached the night of the fight. One was the difficulty of knowing exactly when to launch a raid such as this. Hit the place too early and we may find that nothing criminal had really happened yet. Wait too long and the event could come to an end and the participants start to leave. One great help in countering this problem would be the informant who was willing to attend the fight and wear a body transmitter. We'd have a real-time idea of how things were proceeding.

Another concern was that working with a large force reduced the ability to change plans on the fly. If something unexpected happened, it would be hard to do anything other than stick with the original scheme.

There were quite a few angles to ponder as the time for the raid drew near.

Early in the evening of May 2, I met with and briefed the main part of our arrest force in a meeting room at the Forest Lake Police Department. We had arranged to use several vans and a large U-Haul truck to move our troops into the immediate area of Edward Booth's place when it was time to launch. The State Patrol pilot was asked to hover about a mile away from the location as we moved toward the scene and then sweep in to illuminate the area upon my radio command.

A command post was set up in our motor home at the Chisago City Hall, about seven miles from the target location. Personnel there would keep a log of everything that happened and assist with overall communications.

As the time neared for the dogfights to begin, we received continued updates from two agents hidden in the woods along the only road leading to the target location. They reported a high volume of cars and trucks, all heading toward the suspect's house.

One technical problem we'd had to solve involved the use of a hidden body transmitter by our informant. In 1981, technology lacked many of the refinements of our modern equipment. The device was small and was powered by a nine-volt battery. It put out a weak, limited-range signal that, at best, would reach a few hundred yards. To deal with this, we hid another device called a repeater in the woods within range of the body bug. The repeater, many times more powerful than the body bug, would pick up its weak signal and re-broadcast it to our command post. Someone

was assigned to listen in and tell us periodically what was
going on.

Late in the evening, the actual dog fighting began. We could
discern from the body bug broadcast that there was a raucous
crowd and things were in full swing. I gave the order for our
forces to begin staging a mile or so away from the target house
and to be poised to execute the raid. During the evening the
weather had been deteriorating, and I got word from the
command post that a severe storm cell was forecast to hit the
area within the hour. Almost simultaneously, I was told that
several attendees at the fight were preparing to leave. It was time
to go!

As the vans and the U-Haul were approaching the scene, the
storm cell hit with force. The rain was torrential and the wind
blasted us. Following the plan, the vans and the U-Haul troop
carrier trundled down the country road to the Booth location.
About sixty police officers with riot batons bailed out of the
vehicles and ran toward their assigned positions, surrounding the
dog fight scene. I radioed the helicopter pilot to move in, and
moments later he was hovering overhead. Suddenly, the chopper
pilot turned on his floodlight and, moments later, the aircraft
seemed to tip over on its side, went into a spin, and spiraled off
out of sight. There was a fearsome "Whump!!" sound followed
by complete silence from the helicopter.

It's one thing to sit at a desk and plan strategy for a raid. It's
way more stressful to react on the fly when unexpected disaster
strikes. We had just started when the chopper appeared to crash.
We couldn't see or hear it and had only a vague idea where it had
landed. For several minutes, we had no choice but to deal with
the dogfight crowd. Once we had them subdued and down on the
ground, I quickly broke off a group of officers to look for the
missing chopper and mount a rescue effort. We called on the
command post to send emergency medical first responders and
hoped that there might be someone still alive for them to treat.

With heavy hearts, believing our three officers in the helicopter had probably been killed, we continued to deal with the dog fighters.

Police officers are generally used to scenes of violence and blood. In spite of that, most of us were unprepared for the spectacle we found upon entering the garage where the action was taking place. In the words of Paul McEnroe, a Minneapolis Star reporter who was allowed to accompany us on the raid, "The stunned faces of the police who burst onto the grisly scene held the story of this violent night. In a double garage just after midnight Sunday morning they found blood everywhere; mauled, frightened dogs, bred by their masters to fight or die in pits; and the men and women who revel in it all."

As we entered, two dogs, bloody, with gashed faces and chunks of torn skin hanging from their bodies, were fighting. Their handlers had to use wooden wedges to pry their mouths open and drag them apart to stop the fight. A square fighting pit with about thirty-inch-high walls filled most of the garage. The walls were smeared with blood; the carpeted floor was blood-soaked. One of eight dogs that had fought that night had to be put down immediately. The other seven were taken to an animal hospital, one of them barely alive. All of them were badly torn up—eyes, cheeks, paws, legs, throats. Tied to stakes in the back yard were fourteen pit bulls that had not fought that night.

In all, forty-one people were arrested. Twelve of them, fight promoters and dog handlers, were charged with felonies.

While the fight scene was being processed, I focused my attention on the rescue effort. When last seen, the helicopter had been spinning down toward a lake in a marshy area of the Carlos Avery Wildlife Management Area. Officers ran from house to house along the shore of the lake, pounding on doors, looking for boats to use for the search. They found two. In the words of one searcher quoted in the Minneapolis Star article, "We cruised about ten minutes in open water. Then we tried going through the brush, pulling the boat by grabbing onto branches. Finally, we saw a flashlight shining about 100 yards away."

The flashlight was wielded by John Daniels, one of our lawyers from the State Attorney General's Office. John had come along as an observer on the raid. He'd seen the helicopter spin into the swamp and had been able to mark the direction in which it had fallen. He waded through about a half-mile of frigid muck and icy water until he came to the mangled aircraft. He found all three of the plane's occupants had suffered non-life-threatening injuries but were going into shock. He helped them out of the wreckage and signaled the rescuers who were able to ferry them out in the boat and get them to an ambulance. John, acting on his own initiative, played a key role in saving our three flyers from possible death from exposure. Providentially, the helicopter had crashed on the only type of surface that gave them a chance to survive: a swamp just spongy enough to cushion the fall and water just shallow enough to keep them from drowning.

There was a lot of speculation in the following days about why the helicopter had crashed. There was also criticism of the pilot for flying in the midst of a severe storm. I can only say that he was trying to be a good guy and do what we had asked him to do. No doubt it would have been wiser for him to get out of there when the storm was approaching. When I was able to tell our officers that the three men from the helicopter had been rescued alive, there was a wave of relief.

Never again, from 1981 until I retired in 2003, did I hear of another instance of organized dog fighting in Minnesota. I hope that's an indicator that there are not many people so depraved as to revel in the sights and sounds of animals tearing each other apart.

19

JULIE HOLMQUIST

A young girl sat on the front steps of her home, pulling on her rollerblades, snapping shut each clasp. It was a warm summer evening and she was dressed for exercise in T-shirt and shorts with a small tape player at her waist. This time of year, the days are long in far northern Minnesota and, if she skated hard, she could make it to her turn-around point and home again before dark. She stepped carefully to the street and skated away.

She travelled the few blocks to the edge of her small town, then turned onto the blacktop heading north. Soon she hit her rhythm, a swinging, mile-eating stride. It was a pretty sight, an attractive blond athlete flying down the country road. Everyone who passed in either direction took note of her, remembering in detail where she was and what she looked like. Neither the girl nor those passing could know that she was minutes away from a violent death.

The first time I heard the name Julie Holmquist was on July 30, 1998. Stan Leach, the BCA's resident agent in the Thief River Falls Office, had been contacted by Kittson County Sheriff Ray Hunt. The sheriff had expressed concern over a sixteen-year-old girl who had left her home at about 8:30 P.M. on the previous evening to rollerblade on County Road 1, north of Hallock. The girl had intended to be gone for an hour or so but never returned. The sheriff had done some preliminary checking and was concerned that someone may have abducted the girl, Julie Holmquist. Agent Leach contacted the Bemidji BCA Office for help. During that day, a number of BCA and FBI agents converged on the tiny town in the far northwestern corner of Minnesota. I sent BCA Senior Special Agent Steve Hagenah to coordinate the inquiry.

One of the problems with most abductions is that they are unwitnessed, and no one knows for sure whether a crime has been committed. Absent an obvious scene of struggle, one only knows that there's empty space where there's supposed to be a human being. There's more than one possible reason for a teenager to be missing, but this one looked and felt like a kidnapping, and we treated it as such from the outset.

The first investigative focus was to conduct an extensive canvass of the area in which the girl had intended to skate. Detectives systematically approached people who lived along County Road 1, asking if they had seen her or if they had seen anyone else along the road. If the person making the observation had been driving, the individual was asked for a description of his/her vehicle. Simultaneously, reports began to come in from the public about sightings of Julie or sightings of other vehicles on County Road 1.

There is an art to asking people for their recollections. One needs to understand that people will usually notice and remember the familiar or the very unusual. A person may meet five cars on a country road. If he recognizes one of them as belonging to a neighbor, he will remember it and will probably be able to recall where he met it and whom he saw in the car. If one of the cars is a shiny Model T Ford, he will also remember it but may not have noticed anything about the car's occupants. He may or may not recall anything about the other three—or even that there were three others. As fictional detective Sherlock Holmes famously remarked, "You saw, Watson, but you did not observe."

As the information came in, the investigators began to plot these observations on a map. In doing so, they were able to chart Julie's progress and also note where the sightings ended. Based on the grim reality of past experience, we were working toward locating four sites that may yield critical information:

- A last-seen site
- An abduction site
- A murder site
- A body disposal site

On the map, the agents marked ten reported sightings of Holmquist skating north on County Road 1, all between about 8:30 and 8:50 P.M. Most of these observations were based on the witnesses' general impression of the time. In most cases, it was not possible for them to pin down the exact time at which they had seen Julie, because they'd had no reason to make note of it.

There was one fairly time-specific report by a person who saw Julie approximately four miles north of Hallock, still skating northbound on County Road 1. This witness was hurrying to get to the Cenex Store in Hallock to buy a lottery ticket before the 9:00 P.M. deadline. After interviewing him, the investigators were able to get the video tape from the store for the evening of July 29, 1998. With the witness's help, they located him on the tape at Cenex at 8:59 P.M. Considering that he was driving hurriedly and drove directly to Cenex, they believed that he would have seen Julie about 8:50 P.M. or within a few minutes of that time.

After this sighting, there were two other people who reported seeing Holmquist. One saw her not far south of a bridge over a small stream about five miles north of Hallock; the other saw her a little further on, about 200 yards short of the bridge. It's important to note that all of the witnesses saw the girl skating northward on the county road. No one saw her north of the bridge. We theorized that, if Holmquist had indeed been kidnapped, the abduction site must be near or north of the bridge.

In addition to sightings of an attractive blond girl rollerblading along the blacktop, two witnesses reported making other observations that we later came to regard as important:

> One person was driving north on County Road 1 when he saw Julie. Further along, about 0.6 of a mile beyond the girl, he saw a gray car, stopped along the side of the road. The distance from where the car was stopped to the place later identified as the abduction site is about one mile.

> A witness who was on foot near County Road 1, a few miles north of the abduction site, at about 9:00 P.M. that evening reported seeing a "boxy" gray car traveling north on that road. He noted that one hubcap on the left side of the car was missing, the trunk lid was up, the car was driving on the wrong side of the road, and the driver appeared to be turning around and looking toward the back seat of the car.

While the canvassing effort was going on, a massive search was also underway. Many law enforcement officers and volunteer searchers looked for miles along County Road 1 and the roads that cross it. They paid special attention to the possible abduction area around the bridge. At first the searchers concentrated on looking for Julie herself. They spent days looking in the long grass, the ditches, and field areas along the county roads, and in wooded areas along the general route. Not finding Julie, the search was then directed toward any anomalies along the road. In this effort, every foot of County Road 1—the pavement, the shoulder, and the ditch—were searched from Hallock to an area some miles to the north.

On August 11, 1998, just before dark, searchers found a set of earphones of the sort used with athletic radios and tape players. They were discovered on the east shoulder of County Road 1, a short distance north of the bridge. These earphones were collected and shown to Julie Holmquist's family and friends who said that they were identical to the ones that Julie had used on her tape player.

With the coming of daylight on the following morning, an inch-by-inch search of the site continued. A few feet away from the spot where the earphones had been found, the investigators found and collected two expended .22 caliber shell casings. One looked to have been fairly freshly deposited at the scene. The other was tarnished and appeared to have been there for some time. Having no suspects gun to which the shells could be compared, the officers couldn't know at that time whether either cartridge figured into the kidnapping. They did theorize that a gun may have been fired, either at the girl or near her to scare her into submission.

Also found nearby was a black nylon wrist strap with a metal clip on one end. The subsequent investigation proved that the strap was not an accessory to a tape player such as Holmquist carried. Rather, it was a style supplied with some cell phones.

I spent some time standing by myself at what we now thought of as the abduction site, trying to put myself in the mind of the kidnapper. I always did this at homicide scenes because it helped me to visualize the action and interpret things we found there. The notable thing about the area north of Hallock was the featureless terrain. It's the flattest country I've ever seen. From horizon to horizon there is hardly a dip, and the county blacktop is a straight ribbon that stretches for miles in both directions, finally fading into a mirage at each end. Anyone with a predatory eye toward the young woman gliding along the road would only need one quick scan to know that he could do whatever he wanted with no fear of interruption. I could see him coming upon her in his car to a point of contact. Maybe he stopped, put his window down, and asked for directions—a common ploy that gets the victim to come within striking distance. Maybe he simply swerved close enough to force her off the road, and the rollerblades that worked so smoothly on the pavement became major impediments. Possibly a gun came into play at that point —first as a threat to get her under control, then as a weapon to scare or stop her as she tried to get away.

Of course, it was impossible during this process to avoid also putting myself in the mind of a sixteen-year-old girl who went from endorphin-fed pleasure to adrenaline-charged terror within a few moments. Even though she may have had no time to look around, she would have known that there was no one within miles who could help her.

On August 20, 1998, 22 days after she skated away from home, Julie's body was discovered floating in a shallow pond in a remote gravel pit north of Lancaster, Minnesota. A man looking for a place to bear hunt had found her. She was on her back in the weeds near the edge of the water, just where she would have landed if her killer had carried her over his shoulder to the edge of the bank and toppled her into the pool. Her upper clothing was pulled up around her neck and one arm. Her shorts and underpants were down around one ankle. She was still wearing the rollerblades.

There is no point in graphically describing the condition of the body after more than three weeks of mid-summer weather. I will only note that Julie's skull was missing, most likely carried off by a bear. Her scalp, long blond hair still attached, had slipped free from the skull and was draped across her midsection. After recovering her body, we pumped all of the water out of the pond, looking for any other evidence. Under the body, we found her lower jaw which had probably fallen from the severely decomposed skull as it was pulled away. In the same general area, we found her tape player where it may have been thrown by the killer. The earphones were missing.

Until this time we were investigating a possible abduction case; now we were working a homicide, familiar ground for many of our investigators. There is a way that experience teaches one to think about how and why a crime was committed. I always tried to visualize each part of the crime, beginning with events leading up to it, going on to what the killer may have done afterward. Then I tried to answer this series of questions:

What was the motive? Almost always when women or children are kidnapped, the motive is sexual. In this case the removal of the victim's clothing underscored that probability. Almost certainly the murder was done by one or more men. If a woman took part in the crime (amazingly, this sometimes happens) she would have been subservient to an involved male.

What was the time of death? Because the girl was still wearing her rollerblades, the tape player had been thrown into the pond, and her body was extremely decomposed, it would appear that she had died sometime between initial contact with the killer on the county road and a short time after they arrived at the gravel pit. The interval of time, the environment, and the process of decomposition very effectively destroyed any biological evidence that may have been left by the assailant.

What was the cause of death? Unfortunately, we were never able to answer that question completely. Once we got Julie's body out of the pond, we zipped it into a body bag and I accompanied her to the local hospital where a technician X-rayed the body bag and contents, looking for bullet fragments or other metal items. Finding none, we sent the body to the Ramsey County Medical Examiner in St. Paul for a forensic autopsy. There were two hindrances to a precise determination of cause of death: the missing skull and the severe decomposition. The medical examiner did carefully examine the scalp that had slipped from the skull and found a small hole in the area that would have overlaid the side of the head. Without the underlying skull bone, he couldn't be certain whether it was a bullet hole. We tried very hard to find the skull, including calling out two hundred National Guard soldiers who searched shoulder-to-shoulder over many acres around the gravel pit, but had no success. Knowing a definite cause of death would have let us know if we were searching for a weapon and what kind of evidence we might look for at the murder scene or on the person or clothing of the killer.

Is the gravel pit the murder scene or simply a body disposal site? If the murder wasn't committed near where the body was found, then there would be another site with potential evidence, if only we could find it. We could never be sure of the answer to this question. It's possible that the abduction site was also the murder site.

What can be learned from the way in which this crime was carried out? This looked very much like a crime of opportunity. We didn't expect to find that there was any relationship between killer and victim. Rather, the killer was probably someone who had seen the girl along the road and acted on impulse. The pool of likely suspects, then, would be men who were on the road that evening. It could be someone who lived along the route, saw the girl, and decided to go after her. It could, more likely, be someone who was driving the county road that evening and passed her. He would have a reason to be traveling that route: Maybe he lived there, maybe it was on the way to his destination, or, least likely, he was driving randomly.

It is a unique man who goes from seeing a vulnerable woman to kidnapping and killing her in quick time. Many of the men who passed the girl may have admired her; many may have had sexual thoughts about her, but they kept driving. One person, moved by impulse, careened across the boundaries of society and stopped. He was strong or resourceful enough to overcome an athletic girl and restrain her until he could get her to a private place.

Finally, the place where the girl was brought says something about the killer. Imagine his state of mind after he has rashly confronted the girl, done whatever he had to do to subdue her, and has her in his vehicle. His instinct is to get to the nearest private spot he can find so he can safely finish what he has started. To reach the gravel pit, he drove several miles north, then turned east onto a less travelled road, then north onto an even smaller road. To a person simply driving down the road, the lane leading to the gravel pit doesn't show much promise. One has to open an electric fence, drive across a small cow pasture, and pass through the woods for several hundred yards. It seemed very likely that the killer would have known of this place as he cast about in his mind for a likely spot.

In the early stages of an investigation, when one has developed a rough probable profile of the offender, it's usually helpful to go to the cops who work in the area to ask, "Who comes to mind as a likely suspect in this scenario?" It's sobering when they produce a long list of possible perpetrators. I always thought, *People wouldn't even let their kids go outside if they knew all of the local characters as the police know them.*

Julie's case followed the pattern as we began with a number of local suspects. Added to that, publicity on the case caught the attention of people from the Dakotas down through the Minneapolis/St. Paul area. People in the media always decided how much coverage to give to a case. In Julie's situation, a pretty blond all-American girl, mysteriously abducted and murdered in a tiny farming community, was an irresistible story and they gave it maximum play. The tip-lines rang continuously, each call representing another piece of work for the investigators. Hundreds and hundreds of leads poured in.

On August 31, 1998, Julie Holmquist's funeral was held in an overflowing Lutheran church in Hallock. Not wanting to carry any more emotional distress than necessary, I didn't usually go to funerals for homicide victims. I attended this one. I remained impassive through the service at the church and at the cemetery. Suddenly, at the very end, a cluster of pink and white helium-filled balloons was released and they soared out of sight into the sky. The act was so unexpected and such a dramatic symbol of the girl's spirit flying upward that a collective sob rose from the crowd.

Thank goodness for a pair of dark sunglasses, I thought.

Minnesota Governor Arne Carlson came to the funeral, an unusual sign of interest and respect from a busy state executive. Afterward, back at our command post, I was startled when someone came to tell me that the governor was in the front office and wanted to talk to me. A moment later we stood face to face and he asked me, "Are you going to solve this case?"

All I could think of to say at the moment was, "Governor, we're tough guys but we really care about this case and we're giving it everything we have."

He nodded, turned on his heel, and left. Neither one of us could know at that time that it would be four and a half years until we crossed the finish line.

Through the end of summer and well into the fall, a large group of investigators, led by Senior Special Agent Hagenah, worked seven days a week on the Holmquist Case. There was no public lodging available in Hallock, so at the beginning and end of each long day, they had to make the seventy-mile drive between Thief River Falls and the Kittson County Sheriff's

Office. Piece by piece they winnowed through the leads, one of which they hoped would steer them to the killer.

On October 28, 1998, the unthinkable happened. I received a call from Clearwater County Sheriff Denny Trandem, asking for help with investigating the disappearance of a young woman in his county. We were running on fumes as I pulled most of our people away from the Holmquist investigation to set up a new task force. Five days later the woman's body was found in the woods about twenty miles from her home. We felt we knew what had happened to her, but there wasn't much to go on. Eventually her brother was charged with causing her death, but it took a long time to make the case.

In and around these cases, we continued to have our regular homicides—some easy to solve, some not. In May of 1999, Katie Poirier was kidnapped from her job as a convenience store clerk in Moose Lake, Minnesota, and we began working the biggest case that I ever supervised. The best we could do with the Holmquist investigation was to keep Special Agent Stan Leach out of all of the other activity and let him continue to work in Hallock, partnered with County Investigator Craig Spilde.

Buried in the hundreds of leads that came in during the initial part of the Holmquist Investigation was the name Curtiss Cedergren.

On August 9, 1998, a fourteen-year-old Hallock girl reported that, some time before Holmquist's abduction, the fourteen-year-old had been rollerblading on a rural road when a man driving an older car had slowed down and watched her. She recalled on other occasions having seen the man and the car at the swimming pool in Hallock. By her description of the man and the car, local officers believed that she was describing Curtiss Cedergren.

On August 21, 1998, the day after Julie's body was discovered, the sheriff's department received a call from a landowner. He reported that he had discovered a spot on his property where someone had burned something. A class ring was left in the ashes. A deputy who went out and looked at the burn pile found and retrieved a class ring that was eventually identified as Curtiss Cedergren's. Unfortunately, the deputy was fixated on the class ring and failed to note or collect the burnt material.

In September of 1998, Curtiss Cedergren was interviewed by an investigator and asked about his whereabouts on the night of the Holmquist abduction. He said that he was in Cavalier, North Dakota, on that evening until about 9:15 P.M. and then had driven to his home in Lancaster, Minnesota. His route, according to his statements in that interview, was County Road 1 to County Road 4 to Lancaster.

On June 23, 2000, the Kittson County Sheriff's Office received a complaint from three teen-aged girls who felt that they were being followed by Curtiss Cedergren. They described how, over a three-day period, he had driven behind them with his car in Hallock, parked and watched them at a beach in Lake Bronson, and made several attempts to speak to them. A deputy contacted Cedergren and warned him to stop following the girls.

On July 21, 2000, Leach and Spilde interviewed Curtiss Cedergren. He told the investigators that at the time of the kidnapping he would have been driving a gray Chevrolet Spectrum. He said that he was familiar with Stinar's Pit, the area where Julie's body had been found. He had, in the past, gone swimming and had attended a party there. He also told them that at the time of Julie's abduction he was living in Lancaster. Leach checked motor vehicle records and determined that Cedergren had been the registered owner of a 1987 Chevrolet Spectrum, Minnesota License # BHV 613. The car was a four-door, gray in color.

On July 26, 2000, the investigators spoke with the ex-wife of Curtiss Cedergren. She told them that Curtiss had a pistol and, according to her son, he carried the pistol in his car.

On September 5, 2000, Leach and Spilde spoke with an ex-girlfriend of Cedergren. She recalled seeing a pistol in Curtiss' car. She also said that Curtiss had told her that he was on County Road 1 at the time when Julie disappeared.

As this information continued to come in, Leach and Spilde became more and more interested in Cedergren as a possible suspect. They initiated a trace on the car he had been driving in 1998 and located it in a body shop in Lake of the Woods County. Spilde looked at the car at that location and noticed that it was gray—and that the left front hubcap was missing.

On September 15, 2000, Investigator Spilde took possession of the car and hauled it back to Hallock for forensic examination. He noticed that, as the car was being transported on a trailer, when crossing a railroad track, the car's trunk popped open. He had to secure it with a rope to keep it closed for the remainder of the trip. The car was subsequently processed by BCA forensic experts. Nothing which could physically link the car to Julie Holmquist was found, not terribly surprising considering that more than two years had passed since the kidnapping.

Leach and Spilde obtained records for Curtiss Cedergren's cell phone for the period around the time of Holmquist's abduction. They found that on the night Julie disappeared, five calls were made from Cedergren's cell phone to a number in Cavalier, North Dakota. This number belonged to a woman who was, at that time, Cedergren's girlfriend. Times and duration of these calls were as follows:

- 5:59 P.M. – one minute
- 6:01 P.M. – fourteen minutes
- 6:19 P.M. – nine minutes
- 8:05 P.M. – three minutes
- 8:31 P.M. – nineteen minutes

These calls were placed during the time period in which Cedergren had originally told an investigator that he had been in

Cavalier, North Dakota. They were made from the Hallock area. The investigators spoke with Cedergren's former girlfriend who said that this series of calls was placed when she was breaking off her relationship with Cedergren. The last call, which would have taken place from 8:31 P.M. to 8:50 P.M., corresponds with the time when a witness saw a gray car sitting along County Road 1, about a mile south of the abduction site. When the call ended at 8:50 P.M., Curtiss Cedergren had just been told by his girlfriend that she wanted nothing more to do with him. Simultaneously, Julie was skating northbound near the bridge. About ten minutes later, a car similar to Cedergren's—missing a hubcap and with an open trunk—was seen north of County Road 4, driving on the wrong side of the road with the driver looking into the back seat area.

Left behind, in a spot not far north of where Holmquist was last seen, were her earphones, two .22 shell casings, and a wrist strap from a cell phone.

At this point there was the skeleton of a circumstantial case putting Cedergren at the center of the abduction, but something more was needed. Trace evidence in the form of hairs and fibers vacuumed from Cedergren's car were sent off to the FBI Lab to be examined and compared with samples taken from Julie or her clothing.

On July 16, 2002, Investigators Leach and Spilde asked Curtiss Cedergren to come in for an interview. He agreed to meet with them at the Kittson County Sheriff's Office. They told Curtiss that he was being questioned regarding the Julie Holmquist abduction/homicide. He was shown a photo of the gray Chevrolet Spectrum previously registered to him, and he acknowledged that he had been using that car at the time Julie disappeared. They asked Curtiss whether Julie had ever been in his car; he said she had not. They told him that the car had been processed by forensic experts and trace evidence had been collected and was being analyzed by the FBI Lab. They told him that if his car had been used in the kidnapping, they expected that traces of her would be found. They asked Cedergren if he would be willing to take a polygraph test. He said that he was willing, and Leach told him that he would arrange for the test and would contact Cedergren.

During the first week of August 2002, Leach made numerous calls to Cedergren's phone, attempting to set up the polygraph. He was never able to speak to Cedergren. He left a number of messages, but his calls were never returned.

On August 8, 2002, Agent Leach asked Investigator Spilde to go to Cedergren's house and attempt to arrange for the test. On the following morning, Spilde knocked on Cedergren's front door. A boy answered and Spilde asked if Curtiss was at home. The boy said he would check and left Spilde standing at the front door. Moments later Spilde heard a gunshot from behind the house. He discovered that Curtiss had apparently gone out the back door while Spilde waited in front. Curtiss Cedergren then committed suicide by shooting himself in the head with a shotgun.

After the death of Cedergren had been properly dealt with, Agent Leach and Kittson County Deputies obtained and executed a search warrant on his house. In a closet under some clothing, they found the disassembled parts of a Ruger Mark II stainless .22 caliber semi-automatic pistol. A trace of the gun revealed that it had been purchased at a hardware store in Roseau, Minnesota, by Cedergren.

On November 26, 2002, a BCA firearms examiner determined that the fresh looking expended .22 caliber shell casing found near the earphones at the abduction site had been fired by Cedergren's pistol.

After Curtiss Cedergren's death, an acquaintance of Cedergren came forward to relate a story to Investigator Spilde. The acquaintance said that sometime after the abduction, he had been driving into Hallock with Curtiss as a passenger. As they passed a community sponsored billboard with Holmquist's picture on it, the acquaintance pointed to the sign and asked, "Do you think they will ever get the guy that did it?"

Cedergren replied, "Naw, they will never get him; he'll kill himself first."

The acquaintance said, "Whoever did it would probably get life in the pen."

Curtiss replied, "Before I went to the pen, I would blow my head off."

The practical problem facing us now was this: How could we press our case against a dead man? All of our region, especially the Kittson County area, was still suffering emotionally from the tragedy and trauma that had held everyone's attention for so long. Minnesota has no provision for impaneling a grand jury to hear evidence against a deceased defendant. At this stage, time was definitely not of the essence, so we set on a fairly deliberate course. We first pulled together a group of our seasoned homicide investigators and went over the case in detail. At the end of this review, the unanimous sentiment of this group was that Curtiss Cedergen was our only suspect.

I gave a copy of our case file to one of our experienced criminal prosecutors from the Minnesota Attorney General's Office, asking him to review it. When we met about a week later, I asked him two questions: "If Curtiss Cedergren was still alive, would you be willing to bring charges against him for the murder of Julie Holmquist? And if this went to trial, would you feel you had a strong case?"

He answered, "I'd charge him, and I'd convict him."

On January 14, 2003, we held a press conference at the Hallock City Hall for the announced purpose of discussing the Holmquist Case. It seems silly now, but we had actually wondered whether any media people would bother to make the 366-mile trip from Minneapolis/St. Paul to Hallock. When I drove into town that morning, I saw that the town had been invaded by news people; TV satellite rigs were parked every-where. TV cameras were set up shoulder to shoulder across the back of the room, and there were so many microphones already set up on the podium that I had to rearrange them to make room to lay down my notes. Just before kick-off time, I was visiting with one of the veteran Twin Cities TV reporters who said that this was the biggest press conference he'd ever attended. I had planned for a small, low-key event and found that whatever I said would be broadcast live on WCCO Radio (the big clear-channel station out of Minneapolis) and on TV stations across the Midwest.

The approach we had decided on was simply to lay out the facts of the investigation, not using persuasive language as a lawyer might, just clearly passing on information. Using a PowerPoint presentation, I outlined our investigation, much as I have in these preceding pages, leaving the audience to decide whether Cedergren was the guy. I ended with this statement:

> "After considering the entire body of information gathered in the four and a half years since the crime, the investigators and prosecuting attorneys have concluded that there is considerable reason to believe that Curtiss Cedergren abducted and murdered Julie Holmquist. Conversely, they have no information that leads them to believe that any other person participated in the crime. It would seem that, with what is known today, after thousands upon thousands of investigative hours having been spent, there is nowhere else to go."

A few days after the news conference (and after my heartbeat had returned to normal), I got a call from a Minneapolis news-paper reporter. After a bit of small talk, he said, "I've been getting a lot of E-mails from the public, many of them critical of you guys."

"Do they think we got the wrong person?" I asked.

"No, they're sure you got the right guy; they just can't believe it took you so long to do it," he answered.

That's the way it always seemed to me as well at the end of a case like that one. But the clarity we hoped to experience at the end was hard to find amid the chaos and under the mountain of information that confronted us at the beginning. What we may have lacked in brilliant intellect, though, was usually compensated for with persistent, dogged determination as displayed by Stan Leach and Craig Spilde. That's a common characteristic of homicide investigators, driven by the unforgettable image of a victim, in this case that of a young girl floating in a pond, discarded by a now disinterested predator. We're tough guys, but we really care.

20

THE POIRIER CASE

When Moose Lake, Minnesota, Police Chief Dale Heaton called me in the early morning of May 27, 1999, there was little doubt that he was dealing with a real crime. Police departments get reports of missing people all the time; most of them turn out to be nothing more serious than someone being angry or irresponsible. Heaton described a video tape taken by a gas station security camera showing the clerk, a young woman named Katie Poirier, being taken out of the store by a man holding her from behind. The response I always made on this kind of case was to throw every agent I could spare into the initial effort. By sun-up I already had our three Duluth agents at the scene and more on the way. Among the first arrivals was agent Phill Wagner who, as case agent, would live under the shadow of the Poirier kidnapping for the next fifteen months.

In an abduction case, assessment of the perpetrator's motive is huge and sets the direction of the investigation. We considered three possibilities:

1. It could have been a robbery with the clerk taken to thwart identification of the robber. Even if the female clerk was sexually assaulted in the aftermath, we'd still throw a net over all of the local stickup men if that was the original motivation.

2. It could have been someone from the victim's past or present life who took her for personal reasons—"If I can't have you, no one can"—that kind of situation.

3. Most chilling of all, it could have been a straight-up abduction. The motive would most likely have been sexual. The suspect pool would switch from robbers or disappointed suitors to known or suspected sex offenders.

The surveillance video tape from the Conoco Station where Poirier was taken was grainy and time-lapsed, with jerky movements jumping from one frame to the next. Still, it was a fabulous piece of evidence. It showed the abductor as a white man, medium height, with wavy collar-length hair, wearing a New York Yankees baseball jersey with the number "23." It also allowed us to make some strong deductions about him. This was a bold crime, probably not the work of a novice. Marching a victim from a well-lit store with semi-trucks running in the back lot and customers coming and going was high risk, calling for nerve and confidence.

It appeared that the kidnapper knew how to do this. He had come into the store and walked through the entire business, apparently making sure that no other customers were present. He stepped back outside for a moment, presumably to ensure no one else was around, then went back in. He immediately went to the wash room area, out of sight from the camera. A few moments later, Poirier could be seen walking quickly to that same area, probably in response to some ruse of the kidnapper. A short time later, Poirier, with the man behind her, reappeared and was marched out of the store. When first seen, she had her hands by her throat. As they left the store, she dropped them to her sides and her body language said, "I've given up." It was our feeling that her assailant had choked her into submission in the back room before taking her out. As in any endeavor, a killer, a rapist, or a kidnapper learns by doing. This boldness and the ability to bring a victim quickly under control made us believe that we were dealing with a perpetrator who had done something like this before.

The video tape also helped us to settle on the motive for this crime. It was clear that there was no robbery or theft from the store. It was soon determined that the suspect was not an acquaintance of Poirier's, nor was he known to anybody at the business. Our starting point was that we were dealing with a sexually motivated abduction by an experienced kidnapper. Although we always hoped this one might be the exception, we usually found that the victim had been killed by the time we got the first call. We started out with the sinking feeling that we would be dealing with a homicide committed by a sexual predator, the most difficult category of all of the murders we tried to solve.

One of the reasons we responded in force on a case such as this was the volume of information that had to be gathered before it evaporated. Even when there is a great deal of stealth involved and the killer is unknown in the area, there are few crimes that are committed in a vacuum. The killer comes and goes, drives a vehicle, buys gas, gets coffee, cashes checks, draws money from ATMs, or does any number of other things that are not readily connected to the crime but expose him to the public. There are people who deal with him in different ways who will remember him if they're asked the right questions soon enough after the event. Our method was to capture as much information as possible about who was in the area, what they were doing, and when they were there. Later we would sort it all out.

There are things that take place after a crime has been done. If the perpetrator has killed the victim and disposed of the body, he will move back toward his normal orbit. He may go to where he was before the crime and interact with others. He may also have items he now realizes he needs to get rid of: something of the victim's, bloody clothing, a murder weapon.

One of the things we assigned someone to do fairly quickly was to check garbage. We'd cover not only places in the neighborhood, such as dumpsters and gas station garbage cans, but also routes that a killer may have used in leaving the area. In one of our cases, the victim's body wasn't found for six months, but soon after she disappeared, we found her bloody jacket and purse in a dumpster about ten miles down the road from where she had last been seen.

Almost every little store and gas station has a security video camera in it. Most of these businesses rotate the video recordings. If the recording medium is not pulled out of circulation within a few days, it may be re-recorded. We routinely went to all area businesses that would have been open or had a camera recording during the hours in question and asked for the tapes. This included places in the immediate area and those along logical routes to and from the vicinity. By the following morning we went to every business in town, or in the neighborhood if it was a bigger city, and asked for information that would help to identify anybody who did business there—the day before, the day of, and the time period after the crime. We usually got complete cooperation and were able to look at credit card slips and checks and interview store personnel to get information on anyone they remembered having been in their establishment.

We canvassed the area, just like on the TV cop shows, but

our technique was more pointed and refined. It's important to know what to ask rather than simply, "Did you see anything suspicious?" We systematically covered the area, asking each person, "Who are you? Who else was here at the time in question? Who else did you see in the area, either known or unknown?" If it was a residential neighborhood, we asked, "Who are the people who live or visit on both sides of you?"

As we spoke to people about the Poirier disappearance, one particular set of details caught our attention: reports of a man in a black pickup truck in the Moose Lake area in the hour or so before the abduction. Several people said the man had made them uneasy by his demeanor and the way he looked at women. In interviewing a clerk at the Subway Sandwich Shop adjacent to the Conoco Station, we learned that she had been approached in her business by a man who left when she told him the store was closed. A short time later as she drove off, she saw this man driving in front of her in a black pickup truck. She recalled the partial license plate of 557__Y. We found out later that this was a tremendous lead. At the time, it was one of an avalanche of leads that was already beginning to bury us.

From the onset, those investigations were an organizational challenge, calling for disciplined people to whom big responsibilities could have been delegated. In that case we had an urgent search for a victim we hoped was still alive, the hunt for a kidnapper, and the coordination of a growing number of investigators and the information they were accumulating. All of that in addition to clamoring media people.

A Carlton County Sheriff's Department investigator was given the responsibility of coordinating the hunt for Katie. His directions were to take his crew and search the area around the abduction site to make sure that the kidnapper had not simply taken his victim out into the nearby woods. Once he was positive she was not there, he was to organize a search of all the likely places in the area where a sex offender might take her. When that was completed, he was to begin a series of grid searches, keeping track on a map of all areas checked. This was his assignment for weeks, and he managed the process with a high degree of organization and determination.

Sheriff Dave Seboe agreed to take on the job of dealing with the media, which quickly became a fulltime job. He never has thanked me for suggesting this assignment to him.

On the first evening, we set up our investigative command post in a large basement room at the Carlton County Sheriff's Department. For many days a group of forty or more investigators and support staff started each morning in that room. They received their assignments and hit the street, returning at the end of the day for an evening meeting at which they individually reported on their findings regarding various leads.

In any "Who done it?" type of investigation, we always generated a lot of information as we cast about for the identity of the suspect. Keeping track of details was something we tried to be very disciplined about. We had rigid report writing requirements and analysts and secretaries who were very good at organizing data. When the public got involved in offering information on a case, the amount of minutia increased exponentially and the investigative train would derail if we didn't stay right on top of this. Knowing that we asked for trouble, with a missing victim and an unidentified perpetrator, we had to ask for public input. We hoped that, along with a ton of extraneous nonsense, we'd get one or two gold nuggets of information that would help to break the case.

With the Poirier Investigation there was no choice about public involvement because the media obsessed in a way I had never seen before, even with some of our previous high-profile cases. The best we could do was to make sure that they had good information that would accurately convey what we wanted the public to tell us.

One question we hoped someone could answer for us was, "Who was the guy with the black truck?" We couldn't afford to lock in on him as our main suspect, but we really wanted to talk to him. No one who had seen him had recognized him. There was a fair chance he was from outside the Moose Lake area. In our press releases we put out a description of the truck. We also did something riskier: We had our artist do a sketch of the man—based on witness descriptions—and released it. That sketch made it onto posters, billboards, front pages of newspapers, the ten o'clock news, and the America's Most Wanted Program on national TV. The trouble with composite sketches is they look sort of like everyone but exactly like no one. We got calls from everywhere reporting that the man on the poster was the caller's neighbor, a guy who worked at the carwash, or his ex-brother-in-law. Once we got those leads, even if we were sure they were bogus, we were stuck with them and had to follow up on each one. We also knew that eventually, in court, a defense attorney would hold up our poster to the jurors and ask them to compare our image to the guy with the suit and the new haircut sitting at the defense table.

At one of our morning briefing meetings, FBI Agent Bob Harvey pointed out an important fact for us to consider. He went through a series of well-known national cases like ours and told us that, in each of these investigations, the name of the suspect was known to investigators early on but had been passed over. That turned out to be true in this case as well. One of the obvious things to be done with the Subway clerk's information was to get a computer dump on pickups with license plates matching the partial she had given us. We got the list on the second day of the investigation and found that there were about 2,000 of them. One entry was 557 HDY, listed to a white over gray 1989 Ford pickup belonging to Donald Albin Blom of Richfield, Minnesota, a suburb of Minneapolis. Even though the truck wasn't shown as black, one of our agents asked Richfield officer Beth Roberts to check on the status of this truck. She drove by Blom's house and didn't see the vehicle. When she called the Blom residence she spoke with Mrs. Blom who said that the truck was gray and that Donald had not been driving it as he had loaned it to a friend. At the time, that was enough to move this card to the bottom of the deck.

It's hard to describe the ebb and flow of such a complicated case as days stretch into weeks. The volume of work to be done was enormous; there were 88 leads that came in on suspicious black trucks and 544 on people who looked like the composite sketch. Simply keeping track of this information and the findings of the investigators as they followed up on the leads was difficult. Our analysts had set up a system using standardized lead sheets and specialized software. This helped, but we still wore out a lot of shoe leather as we attempted to prove not only who did this crime but who didn't do it.

On Friday, June 18, 1999, the twenty-second day since the kidnapping, Carlton County Sgt. Kevin Mangan began following up on lead #1960. He spoke with an employee of the Minnesota Veterans' Home in Minneapolis who had reported that Donald Hutchinson, a fellow employee, looked like the composite, wore a Yankees jersey like that of the kidnapper, and drove a black truck. He also said that Hutchinson had not come to work on the morning after the kidnapping, had radically changed his appearance, and had quit driving his pickup.

A records check revealed that Donald Hutchinson had changed his name to Donald Blom, a name already in our indices in the list of truck owners. His criminal history listed fourteen aliases and a string of arrests for kidnapping and sexually assaulting young women. Unfortunately, his name hadn't been included in our roster of registered sex offenders, since the registration law was enacted after his last arrest. Blom's forte was grabbing women in public and forcing them into his vehicle. He controlled his victims by choking them into submission.

We had planned to shut down the investigation for two days that Saturday and Sunday because it was Grandma's Marathon weekend in Duluth and there wasn't a motel room available for miles. Instead, we embarked on a marathon of our own. Carlton County records revealed that Donald and Amy Blom owned twenty acres of country property near the tiny town of Kerrick, not too many miles from the site of the abduction. We already knew about the Richfield address. As the night wore on, we drafted search warrants for both places.

At 1:33 A.M. on Saturday, Carlton County Sergeants Mangan and Timm, with a signed search warrant, entered the mobile home on Blom's rural property looking for a living Katie Poirier. Not finding what they had hoped for, they left other officers at the scene to wait for the BCA Lab crime scene team.

At 8:45 A.M., BCA and FBI agents, along with Richfield officers, went to the Blom residence with a search warrant. The Bloms were not there; a neighbor said they were camping in northern Minnesota. Parked in the locked garage, the agents found a 1989 Ford pickup, license # 557 HDY. It was not gray, as Amy Blom had said—it was black.

Through the day investigators worked with the crime scene team as they combed the rural Blom property for evidence. It's a tribute to their thoroughness that, with no information which would cause them to suspect Poirier's body may have been burned, they sifted the ashes in an outdoor fire pit. There they found charred bone fragments, later categorized by forensic anthropologist Susan Myster as those of a young woman, burned while there was still flesh on the bones. The pieces of bone, most about the size of a quarter, were too badly burned to allow for DNA extraction. They came from various parts of a human skeleton and represented an entire person. Among these pieces was a human jaw fragment and corresponding tooth which odontologist Ann Norrlander ultimately identified, "to a degree of medical certainty" as that of Kathlyn Poirier. An image that will forever haunt me is a photo of the fire pit as we found it, with two lawn chairs nearby. I imagine Donald Blom sitting there in the middle of the night, calmly feeding boards onto Katie Poirier's funeral pyre.

While the fire pit was being sifted, other investigators were working on finding Donald Blom. On Saturday evening, he was located camping with his family near Alexandria, Minnesota.

At 12:10 A.M. on Sunday, June 20, 1999, BCA Agent Phil Hodapp knocked on the door frame of Blom's camper. In the interview that followed, Blom told Hodapp a number of lies. Not knowing that his black Ford truck was already in the evidence bay at the BCA, Blom said that he had last seen the truck on May 15 when he'd sold it to his brother. After the interview, surveillance was done on Blom. He was arrested as he and his family returned to their Richfield home.

During the succeeding months, the most thorough investigation I had ever been a part of continued to flesh out the information on Blom. Our case agent, Phill Wagner, along with Marv Durkee from the sheriff's department and Bob Harvey from the FBI, continued to head up the northern task force. BCA's Joel Kohout and the FBI's Lynn Tremaine led a second task force in the Twin Cities. Tracking Blom's financial activities, we made these discoveries:

Blom wrote a check for a haircut, dating it May 23, three days before the kidnapping. It was established that the barber shop was closed that day. Deposit records from the shop indicated that the haircut took place after the kidnapping. The barber recalled that Blom asked to have his hair cut much shorter than usual.

Debit records showed that Blom made purchases at a Menard's store on May 21 and 22, 1999. Using this information, investigators were able to get security video tapes from Menard's showing what Blom looked like several days before the kidnapping. One particular shot of Blom was from an angle similar to that of a camera at the kidnapping scene, and it showed a remarkable likeness between Blom and the suspect.

Debit records showed that Blom had made a purchase at Banning Junction, about fifteen miles south of the kidnapping site, at 5:15 P.M. on the evening of the kidnapping.

A sales slip in Blom's truck showed a purchase at Charlie's IGA in Moose Lake on May 25, 1999. This was one of the sites where witnesses had reported the suspicious man with the black truck.

A meat label on a package of hamburger in Blom's mobile home was traced to Holiday Foods in Moose Lake and would have been sold on May 25, 1999.

Several other helpful facts came to light as the investigation continued:

Mark Blom, Amy Blom's brother, told us that he had purchased a Yankees jersey with the number 23 and a Cardinals jersey while attending a game at Yankee Stadium. He had later given both jerseys to Donald Blom. The Yankees jersey, similar to the one worn by the kidnapper, was never found. The Cardinals jersey was found during the search of Blom's house in Richfield.

Even though Amy Blom claimed that Donald was in Richfield with her on the night of the kidnapping, phone records showed that several phone calls were placed from their home in Richfield to the supposedly vacant mobile home up north. From the duration of the calls, it appeared that no connection was made. The theory was that Donald was missing and Amy was looking for him.

Video tape from a camera shooting through the window of a gas station in downtown Moose Lake showed a truck

identical to Blom's, passing by on the street about an hour
before the kidnapping.

These few highlights afford just an idea of the thoroughness
of the Poirier investigation. The case was represented by a shelf
in an analyst's office with about six feet of file folders; 2,986
leads were covered.

Donald Blom was tried and convicted of the murder of Katie
Poirier during the summer of 2000. When the verdict came back,
I felt as if a thousand pounds had been lifted from me.

Entering into the investigation, knowing in my heart that
Katie had to be dead, I had the same feeling I'd had many times
at homicide scenes. The last brutalized remains of the victim
spoke not just of the mechanics of what was done, but the cold-
ness or rage, or sheer malevolence of the killer. There was only
one thing left that could be done for such a person who was
beyond any other help: Find the one who brought this life to a
premature end.

There was a lot of satisfaction in having worked hard and
solved a terrible crime. Beyond that, there wasn't much that was
positive in the Poirier case. It was tragic that a promising young
woman never got to marry or have children or experience matu-
rity. It wasn't fair that a family lost one of its young members to
an untimely death at the heedless whim of a stranger. It didn't
seem right that Blom's family had to live under the pall of
infamy that he cast upon them. It was a shame for Donald Blom,
himself, that he was unwilling or unable to fight off the evil
impulse that triggered this chain of events.

As I write this, Donald Blom sits in a maximum-security
prison. He'll die there, and that's as it should be. He's a strong
suspect in the murder of another young woman a few years
before Poirier, although that case was never made. While examining the bone fragments from the fire pit, the anthropologist set
aside one bone, saying that it was human, but didn't match with

Poirier's. We were never able to learn the origin of that bone. Considering Blom's past offenses, his actions in this case, and his probable involvement in other crimes, it's no stretch to say that putting him away may have saved more than one woman's life.

21

GUNS

W hen I was growing up in northern Minnesota, we always had a few guns around the house. There was a Japanese 7.7mm rifle, complete with bayo-net, that Dad had brought back from the war. At age seventeen I found I could get ammo for it and started using it for deer hunt-ing, minus the bayonet. My brother had an odd make foreign rifle—Russian, I think—that he'd picked up for a few bucks at the hardware store where they had a barrel full of them. We each had single-shot shotguns we used for partridge hunting. Dad was our gun safety instructor and hunting coach. He'd grown up on a remote homestead just south of the Canadian border where hunting was the key to having food on the table. I've had more dietary options in my life than my father did in those early days, but I have faithfully followed his rule that you never hunt for anything you don't intend to eat.

We didn't love our guns any more than one would love a hammer or a screw driver. Like any other useful implement, we liked having them when we needed them and took good care of them. We also had great respect for them, both from Dad's coaching and from simply observing the devastating effect they had on the creatures we hunted. Even though I've handled guns almost every day of my adult life, I've never come close to being injured by one that I was holding.

My entry into the police world moved me into a new phase that continued all through my working life, one in which guns were the primary tools of my trade. On my first day on the job, the department issued me a Smith and Wesson .38 special revolver, the gun carried by almost all cops of that era. I doubt that I had ever shot a pistol of any kind before that time, but I practiced shooting a lot and the gun became second nature to me. Knowing that your life may depend on getting your gun out fast and hitting what you intend to hit is plenty incentive to work hard on weapon proficiency. With a revolver, reloading is a slower proposition than it is with modern semi-automatics. The .38s we carried held six rounds in the cylinder. When they were gone you flipped the cylinder open, pushed an ejector rod to dump the empty casings, and fed new shells individually into place. In addition to the extra ammo I carried on my belt, I always had six rounds in my right front pants pocket for the first reload. When they were used up, it might have been time for a new strategy. I think the first time I ever pointed that gun at anyone was when I came across a broken window in a business place late one night, sauntered up on foot to take a look, and came face-to-face with a burglar, lying on the floor looking up at me. You should have seen my quick draw!

The other gun that was available to me when I was on duty was a 12-gauge pump shotgun in a mount attached to the center of the dash in the squad car. It was always loaded with four rounds of double-ought buckshot, pellets about the size of a small pea. We fired these guns a lot on the range, and even those of us who had grown up with shotguns had usually had enough after fifteen or twenty rounds. Our shoulders would be black and blue for a week after the experience. If you knew you were going to get into a shoot-out, that was your weapon of choice.

When I went to work in the Organized Crime Unit, we were expected to provide our own pistol. I went to Warner Hardware in downtown Minneapolis and bought a Smith and Wesson Model 19 .357 magnum revolver, still my all-time favorite handgun. As the term "magnum" would indicate, this gun packed quite a bit more punch, greater penetration, and more stopping power than the .38. It was my primary handgun for about the next decade; then everything changed.

In the early 1980s, the police world, at least my part of it, was transitioning to semi-automatic pistols. The advantage of these guns over revolvers is greater bullet capacity and quicker reloading capability. We were issued Smith and Wesson 469 9mm's. They carried 12 rounds in a magazine with one more in the chamber. To reload, one simply dropped the empty clip, slammed another into place, released the slide, and you were back in business. We had several days of transition training when we did the switch-over. The thing that I found especially worrisome was how most of the first day was spent teaching us what to do when the gun malfunctioned. In my entire career to this point, I was only aware of one revolver malfunction, the time that one of the Bloomington officers used a hand-loaded bullet with many times the proper amount of powder in it and blew out the whole side of the cylinder. While it is true that semi-autos are more susceptible to jams than revolvers, constant training and practice eventually won me over to consider them my handgun of choice.

There were special purpose weapons, used by our dynamic entry teams and SWAT officers. The M16, a fully automatic military rifle, was our medium-distance gun. For close-up fire power, we used H & K MP5s, 9mm fully automatic short-barreled rifles carried by a sling around the shooter's neck. Both of these styles of automatics had selector switches that allowed the operator to choose to fire a single shot or a magazine-emptying stream of fire. Other than trying it out on the firing range to see what it felt like, I suspect that few non-military people have used a weapon on full "rock and roll" since Al Capone's boys hosed down their adversaries with their Thompson sub-machine guns. Law enforcement people need to think about where every round they fire is going, and a wandering fusillade of lethal missiles is almost never a good idea. The unique thing about our MP5s was that they each had a suppressor on the end of the barrel that muffled the report so efficiently that the loudest sound one heard while shooting was the bolt clacking back and forth.

During my last twenty years on the job, we went through two further generations of handguns: Beretta 9mm's and Sig Sauer .40 calibers. Now most of the cops I know carry Glocks, Austrian-made pistols known for simple construction and trouble-free operation.

The technical part of all of that was straight-forward: You train and train to raise your familiarity and skill to the highest possible level, one at which, no matter the stress level, you'd be able to make it work. There's tension between several elements of the moral, ethical, philosophical considerations of cops using guns. No right-thinking person wants to shoot another human being. No non-suicidal man or woman wants to be shot, especially after seeing a few gunshot victims first hand. With no warning a cop may find himself in a place where one of these two things will take place.

One can't get far into a police career without reflecting on the question, *If I have to shoot someone, am I willing to do it?* If the answer is *No,* then it's time to go into another profession.

The daily permutations of the police job frequently put an officer in situations that could spin into one where shooting is unavoidable. Statistically that happens very infrequently, a testament to the abilities of most cops to navigate dangerous situations and resolve them without resorting to deadly force. How many times did I have my gun out, ready to shoot if there was no alternative? I don't know—many, many times. The people I worked with and I arrested murderers, rapists, armed robbers, big time drug dealers—men and a few women with all types of weapons and violent intentions. We took risks and stretched our luck to the limit to avoid shooting. A few times one of us did pull the trigger.

When I was a young uniformed officer, my routine was to load my revolver and put it in my holster just before I left for work and unload it upon arriving home. With young kids in the house, I didn't want to leave a loaded gun around. One night I arrived home after a busy shift, opened the cylinder of my revolver, and, to my horror, saw that it was empty. I remembered being distracted as I was leaving for work earlier and I must have put the gun in my holster thinking to load it in a moment and then forgot. I spent some time thinking about all of the calls I'd been on during the previous eight hours and felt relieved that none of them had led to a shooting situation.

I'm very thankful to say that I was able to cross the finish line of my career without having to shoot anyone. I'm also thankful that the one time someone shot at me, he missed.

22

SHOOTOUT AT THE TURTLE CLUB

I was sleeping soundly when the phone by my bedside rang. It was about 1:30 A.M. on December 27, 1992. The call was from an unusually agitated dispatcher at the Beltrami County Sheriff's Office who said that there had been multiple shots fired at the Turtle Club Bar, about ten miles north of Bemidji. Several people were believed to have been killed or wounded. There were deputies at or arriving at the scene, and the dispatcher was unsure whether any of them had been shot. Sheriff Dwight Stewart had requested immediate help from the BCA.

Even with the sketchy information I'd been given, it was clear that a major response was called for. A shooting in a bar meant there'd be multiple witnesses to interview and a complicated crime scene to process. The possibility of several victims added to the complexity. I called out all of the BCA's complement of agents in the Bemidji area, told my drowsy wife I'd see her later, and headed for the Turtle Club. While enroute, I was able to communicate with Beltrami County by radio and confirm that there were dead and wounded victims at the scene but that the situation had been stabilized by the sheriff's department.

The Turtle Club was in a rural setting along Highway 71, a rustic looking building set among the trees about a block from the highway. As I turned onto the driveway, I saw a squad car parked on the road and a pickup truck that had been driven into the deep snow just opposite the police car. As I got closer, I saw a deputy by the squad car; he seemed to be standing guard over the truck. I parked behind his squad and walked to the officer. As I approached, I was able to see several bullet holes in the driver's side of the truck; the left front door was open, and a man was slumped behind the wheel. By this time in my career, I'd seen enough dead bodies to know what I was looking at.

The deputy gave me a chilling account of what had happened not long before I got there. A number of officers had been dispatched but he was the first one on the scene. With little information, other than that people had been shot and there was still an active shooter at the bar, he parked his squad at the edge of the parking lot, took his shotgun and approached the front of the building on foot, using the cover of some nearby trees. To his horror, he saw a man with a pistol in his hand exit the front door of the bar, walk to a person who had been crawling, apparently injured, in the parking lot, and shoot that person in the head. The shooter then got into his pickup and began to career out of the parking lot. The deputy, still on foot, leveled his shotgun at the truck, trying unsuccessfully to get the driver to stop. As the pickup roared by him, the officer emptied his shotgun at it, flattening the front tire and, possibly, wounding the driver. The truck went off the road into the deep snow, and the officer approached from the driver's side with his handgun in combat position. When it appeared that the man in the pickup was trying to bring his pistol to bear on the deputy, the officer shot and killed him.

No one who has any inkling of the internal trauma and emotion present in this kind of officer-involved shooting would think it appropriate to leave that officer guarding the scene. Within a few minutes I found another deputy to relieve him.

The situation at the bar was controlled but still chaotic. Two dead men lay in the parking area near the front door. Two other men had been shot and wounded and had already been transported to the hospital.

Working with the sheriff, I began to organize the complicated situation into manageable parts. There were about thirty traumatized people in the building, some of them intoxicated. We arranged to take all of them in a school bus to the law enforcement center to be interviewed. I sent several agents there to take statements.

The crime scene encompassed the entire inside of the bar, the parking lot with two bodies, an area with a blood trail and shell casings in the snow behind the building, and the pickup truck with the shooter's body in it. We arranged to have deputies secure the scene, and I called our BCA Lab crime scene team to come and process it. At that time the team came out of the St. Paul Office, so we knew it would be well into morning before they got there.

This was also an officer-involved shooting situation, adding another dimension to the case. Typically, the BCA handles that with no involvement by the local jurisdiction. The officer was asked to give his account on the record, ballistics of weapons used were compared, any witnesses to that part of the case were interviewed, and ultimately the county attorney would decide if the shooting was justified. Several agents were given the assignment.

With things under control at the Turtle Club, I went to the law enforcement center. Because there was a backlog of people to be interviewed, I began to help with that part of the investigation. The first person I interviewed was a woman who said she was worried about her husband. Although she had tried to stop him, he had gone out the front door of the bar, intending to subdue the shooter. She hadn't seen him since.

"What was he wearing?" I asked her. When she described his

clothing, I had to give her the news that her husband was one of the men who had been shot to death in the parking lot.

By morning we had pieced together an account of what had happened at the bar. The shooter, the man I had seen dead in the pickup truck, was Delwyn Dudley, a lieutenant with the Red Lake Reservation Police Department. By all accounts, under normal circumstances, he was a good man, well-liked by his peers. About 9:30 in the evening, Dudley had come into the bar and had a confrontation with a group of people, including his estranged wife and Darrell Lussier, a member of the Red Lake Tribe and a former Beltrami County Deputy. Dudley accused his wife and Lussier of having a romantic affair. When the dispute became noisy, Dudley was told by the bar manager to leave and he did so.

At about 12:45 A.M., Dudley re-entered the bar, walked to the table where his wife and a group of women were sitting, and pulled a 9mm handgun from his waistband. When he pointed the pistol at Lussier, who was seated nearby, one of the women grabbed Dudley's gun arm while Lussier ran out of the bar. A male patron approached Dudley, apparently to intervene, and was shot in the abdomen and gravely wounded. Dudley briefly left the bar and it appeared he must have found Lussier outside where he shot and wounded him. He probably believed that he had killed him. We later found tracks in the snow and a blood trail showing that Lussier had crawled all the way around the building and back into the parking lot after having been shot. At about this same time, the man whose wife I had interviewed exited the front door, confronted the shooter, and was fatally shot in the chest. As this was happening the sheriff's dispatchers began to receive their first frantic calls from the bar.

Moments later, Delwyn Dudley re-entered the building, this time carrying an AR-15 semi-automatic rifle. He opened fire, spraying shots randomly around the building. Some people hit the floor, hiding behind overturned tables. Others hid in a beer cooler or ran out a back door into the woods. Remarkably, only one more person was wounded during this barrage. Dudley exited the front door of the bar at that point and found Darrell Lussier crawling in the parking lot, fatally shot him, and drove away to his final encounter with the deputy.

Our lab team spent several days processing the scene. They found that 21 rounds had been fired inside the bar and 13 outside. In those days they marked bullet trajectories by stretching strings from the point of impact back to the point of origin. When I looked at the 21 strings fanning out across the barroom, my first reaction was surprise and thanks that more people had not been shot.

That type of incident leaves a lot of trauma in its wake. Obviously, the people who were there and experienced all of this violence firsthand were dramatically affected. The police dispatchers who took the first calls for help and then listened to ten or fifteen minutes of gunshots and people screaming over a phone that had been left off the hook were badly shaken by the sounds they heard, especially knowing they had a deputy at the scene who had dropped out of contact. In the aftermath, members of the sheriff's department grieved for Darrell Lussier who had worked with them from 1974 to 1986. The officer who brought everything to an end will never forget seeing Lussier executed in the parking lot and the fear and adrenaline rush of his wild encounter with the killer. As often happens with police officers who are involved in shooting situations, he moved on to another job. I never saw his name in the media and I won't name him here. I even feel a little sad when I remember putting my hand on a woman's shoulder to tell her that the husband she was worried about was one of the men who had been killed in the parking lot.

Where did Delwyn Dudley think he was going as he began to roar out of the parking lot? The immediate answer, of course, was away from the Turtle Club. He'd had the fight and now his main impulse was flight. But where could he have gone? My hunch was that when he went back into the bar with his guns, he had, at least temporarily, passed the point of caring about anything except getting revenge for the way he felt he'd been wronged. However, even as he got into his truck, he would have known that this was a one act play that would end in tragedy for him as it had for his victims. Had he gotten away, it's my hunch that he would have soon thereafter died, either by his own hand or by suicide by cop as we tried to arrest him.

A few years after that night of violence, the Turtle Club was torn down. I don't know if the business fell apart, the memories were too unpleasant, or some other factors came into play. Now it's just a peaceful spot in the country showing no evidence that one wild night, bullets flew and people died there.

23

THE RIOT

A t the beginning of September 1989, I was given an assignment I didn't want. I was Special Agent in Charge of the BCA's Bemidji Regional Office. We had a full plate of homicide and serious drug investigations. I had important things pulling at me from every direction. It was not at all exciting to have BCA Superintendent Mark Shields call and tell me to put a team of agents together and head for International Falls, Minnesota, to respond to a request for assistance from Koochiching County Sheriff Bill Elliot.

The assignment was to provide technical assistance in monitoring a labor protest rally to be held as part of a dispute between construction labor unions and the Boise Cascade Paper Mill. Local law enforcement was hearing rumblings that there would be trouble. I was to set up a system to videotape the action and, if violence did occur, to identify those responsible from either side of the dispute.

International Falls is a small community situated right at the top of Minnesota, an easy rifle shot from Canada. Most people think of it as a way-station on the threshold to wilderness adven-

ture. Seven days a week, trucks pulling boats or loaded down
with hunting equipment form a line at the border crossing. Local
businesses provide last minute supplies. Anyone passing through
quickly notices that "The Falls" is dominated by the paper mill,
which reputedly employs about 10% of the town's population.

At the center of the dispute was the $535 million expansion
of the mill, an improvement that was expected to bring hundreds
of additional jobs to the small community. B E & K, a Birming-
ham, Alabama, construction company, had been selected to build
the addition, based on a bid that was about $40 million less than
the nearest competitor. B E & K had a reputation for using non-
union labor. This selection on such a large project enraged labor
leaders in Minnesota, a traditional stronghold of organized labor.
As construction proceeded during the spring and summer, union
sub-contractors worked alongside B E & K workers in a kind of
tense accommodation. Then, on July 18, 150 union workers,
demanding more union worker participation, walked off the job,
creating a standoff. Work continued with about 500 non-union
employees, many of whom were easily identified in the community by their southern accents. Some local businesses profited
from this influx of visitors and, presumably, were glad they had
come. Other citizens, sympathetic to the union view, resented the
outsiders. These dynamics put International Falls into a state of
trouble waiting to happen.

Because the town didn't have adequate housing available for
the out-of-towners, a "man camp" had been established a mile or
so from the mill. This was a veritable city of trailer houses
surrounded by high cyclone fencing with heavy duty gates,
patrolled by private security guards. Many of the B E & K
workers lived there. Rumor was that the protest rally would take
place in front of this housing area, the most vivid symbol of non-
union participation in the building project.

I went to International Falls a few days before the anticipated rally to scope out the territory. I found a large, several story building under construction about a hundred yards away from the man camp. A second-floor window opening provided a good view of the street, the front fence, and the outer rows of trailers. I planned to put a couple of agents there to get over-all video and be able to zoom in on activity that might be of interest. I decided to put a team of agents in plain sight right on the street in the front of the complex. Dressed in civilian clothes and using professional looking video equipment, people could easily presume they were TV news people. I would put myself, with radio communications beside the camera operators and local police, in the middle of the action as it developed.

As the day of the rally neared, Sheriff Elliot became increasingly concerned as he continued to get information that planners of the rally were anticipating more than just peaceful protest. Union supporters from out of town were expected to show up -- an unknown but possibly large number of them. Elliot contacted Minnesota Governor Rudy Perpich to request help from the National Guard. Perpich, a DFL politician from the Iron Range, ground zero for union sympathy in the state, declined. The best that Elliot would be able to do was to ask for whatever help he could get from neighboring county law enforcement. All workers who had been living at the man camp were evacuated, leaving in place just a small force of security guards.

Early in the morning of Saturday, September 9, a force of about forty-five officers, drawn from the International Falls Police Department and the Koochiching and St. Louis County Sheriffs' Departments, was in place. As protesters began to arrive, we noticed that many of them were parking their vehicles in a parking lot across a highway about a block from the man camp and walking to the rally site. I had my on-the-street camera men film these people as they streamed in. The protesters largely ignored the cameras, probably assuming they were news reporters. As the group in front of the man camp swelled, the sheriff's department received word that three coach-type busses, full of union iron workers from Michigan, had just rolled into town and would be dropping off all of their passengers at the rally. I later heard news reports estimating anywhere from 400 to 600 protesters were in attendance when the rally got into full swing. Whatever the number, it was quickly apparent that, if things got out of hand, the crowd was far too large for a small number of cops to handle.

I was standing on the edge of the street, just across from the man camp fence, as the crowd began to build. Two things immediately stood out to me: One was that it was a very surly crowd, not really surprising, at a protest; the other was that a sort of beery breeze seemed to waft over the group. It was apparent that many of the attendees had afforded themselves a liquid breakfast, a practice that never has a calming effect on people in conflict. The uniformed police officers were mostly stationed along the perimeter fence, facing the crowd. The sheriff had left his personal pickup truck parked along the curb near where I was standing and had bravely gone to try to identify any obvious protest leaders and engage with them. It soon became evident that he was wasting his effort.

The crowd had reached its full size, and individual anger began to swell into group rage. It started with shouts and curses. Soon some individuals were throwing rocks, which it appeared they had brought with them, at the front row of trailer houses. The crowd surged forward, and there was little the officers could do about it. Hundreds of protesters pressed up to the fence, pushing and pulling on it. At first the fence looked as if it would hold, but as the pushers and pullers got into rhythm with each other, I could see that it was going down. In moments, the fence was flat and the crowd roared as they pushed into the compound, smashing windows and kicking in the doors of the nearest trailers.

Suddenly there was a wild piece of action that seemed to freeze everyone for a few moments. A station wagon came from the rear of the compound and raced toward a padlocked gate at a secondary entrance about 200 feet down the fence line from where the main crowd was misbehaving. It was the security guards who had decided to make a break for it. Instead of slowing, as they approached their exit point, the car sped up. They hit the heavy-duty chain link gate at about forty miles per hour, crashed on through, made a right turn, and raced off out of sight with a good part of the gate hanging over both sides of the car.

As the action continued, it was evident that some of the protesters had come prepared to cause maximum damage in the man camp. Groups of men overturned vehicles inside the fence, smashed trailer windows, and systematically set the trailers on fire. Groups of police officers engaged in hand-to-hand combat with some of the demonstrators. The protest had turned into a riot.

A mob is an ugly thing, in part because of the hatred it acts out, also for the aggressiveness it fosters that wouldn't be there with an individual. As many of the protesters wreaked vengeance on the man camp, others in groups looked for anything else they could do to cause trouble. Seven or eight men, led by a bandy-legged little guy with beer on his breath, swaggered up to me. "Who are you?" the leader asked me.

"I'm a police officer," I replied.

Turning to his group he said, "Maybe we should turn his truck over, boys!"

"That would be a big mistake," I said. "That's the sheriff's truck, and you guys would be in a lot of trouble if you wrecked it."

Probably sensing that he was losing his followers, who didn't seem enthused about getting crosswise with the sheriff, he sneered and turned away, and the group wandered off.

It's difficult to say how long the riot lasted. There's no sense of time with that much action happening. Eventually there was nothing left to wreck; black smoke billowed up from the burning trailers and cars. The damage was later estimated at $1.3 million. The police had been able to arrest a handful of people; the rest all headed back to their cars and home, feeling however people feel after doing something that violent and destructive.

The iron workers from Michigan got on their buses, confident in their anonymity. At this point, we had a bright idea: We would stop the busses and see if any of the police officers could identify any individuals who had done specific criminal acts. With the State Patrol's help, we turned the busses around and had them drive to the law enforcement center. There, with most of the officers who'd been at the man camp observing, we unloaded the busses, one person at a time. Some of the men couldn't be identified with any criminal act. Many others, though, seemed to wilt and shrivel up as they heard an officer say, "I want that guy!" No longer part of a mob, they were pretty mild. All in all, 32 people were arrested and booked before the remainder were allowed to head for home.

What had started out as a simple assignment now became a complicated investigation that went on for weeks. We reviewed video tapes to pick out specific criminal action, like lighting fires or smashing windows, and to get the best images we could find of the people involved. We compared these pictures with close-up video our men on the street had shot as the protesters were arriving. We had copied all the license numbers of protesters who'd parked in the area of the man camp and now were able to compare vehicle registration information and driver's license photos with the images we had captured. Then, one by one, we picked them off, got arrest warrants, and brought them into custody. I don't remember what the final count was. Most of them were a lot meeker when dealt with as individuals than they had been as part of a mob.

I have no opinion as to the validity of the union workers'

complaints against the paper company. People with a union background would probably feel that their anger, if not their actions, was justified. Others who back a merit shop system would disagree. I only know that the riot was one of the ugliest things I have ever seen.

COURAGE

C ops come in an array of human packages. The stereotypical ones are big and strong enough to discourage most sober, sane people from tangling with them. There are a lot of others who don't fit this mold at all: men who are not imposing, women who would be at great physical disadvantage in a fight with a more powerful male, mild-mannered guys with glasses—more Clark Kent than Superman. All of these people can be successful police officers if they have one vital characteristic: courage. Without it, the Incredible Hulk wouldn't belong in a police uniform. With it, pretty average people can do the job.

It takes courage to get into a squad car, knowing that a few terse words from a police dispatcher may send you to handle an impossible situation. As the shift goes on, you may encounter only the mundane or you might suddenly rush to deal with violence, bloodshed, or death. You may be the first one to arrive at a terrible accident and be responsible for knowing what to do while surrounded by hysterical people.

One needs courage to use restraint when dealing with violent, threatening suspects. I and the people I worked with took every imaginable kind of personal weapon away from people, some in hand-to-hand combat, at great peril to our own lives. It would have been safer for us to keep our distance and immediately use deadly force. Instead, we reasoned or cajoled or commanded; we engaged with less than lethal weapons like Mace or a baton or a chair. Even all these years later, I can call up in my mind a sort of closed-loop video replay of some of these situations and am as happy now as I was then that I survived them.

It takes intestinal fortitude to tell people what they don't want to hear: "You're under arrest." "You're getting a speeding ticket." "I have to tell you your son was killed in a car accident." There were few opportunities to give someone a positive message. Even "We've arrested the man who murdered your daughter" has so much grief attached that it's not at all uplifting.

Courage is needed to propel an officer toward a scene that everyone else is running away from. If you were at the mall and were suddenly confronted by a crazed man brandishing a gun, you would have several options. If you were feeling particularly good about yourself, you could decide to take him on. Few would make that choice. You could fall back to what you considered a safe distance, call 911, and try to vector in the first responders. Or you could simply do what most people do and run like your pants were on fire. An officer who gets this call has only one option: Rush to the mall, run toward the sound of shots fired, and take on whatever he finds the situation to be. He does this knowing that he may have to kill or that he may, himself, die. He also knows that, in the succeeding days, people will review video from security cameras and cell phones, examining the action from every angle, and make proclamations on how he did. You have to be brave to do this job.

Especially nowadays, when there seems to be so much venom directed toward cops, the uniformed officers hit the street each shift knowing that any call can be a setup for an ambush. This has to be on their minds a lot. It's not a completely new phenomenon, though. Even in my time, in 1970, St. Paul Officer James Sackett was shot to death as he answered a bogus call that a woman in labor needed help. It was a set-up all the way. The people who drive the marked squads know this is a possibility, but they respond to all of their calls anyway. We hear of ethnic areas in some European cities that are "no go zones," neighborhoods the police will not enter. Until recently this would have been unimaginable in the United States. Now there actually are such areas in Seattle, Portland, and Minneapolis. It was local politicians, not cops, who decided to allow this.

Whenever an officer is involved in a shooting situation, whether as the shooter or the victim, the newspaper editorial pages will light up. Some will comment sympathetically on the dangers involved in policing. Inevitably, at least one writer will point out that there are many other more dangerous professions. Statistically, that's certainly true; there are more loggers, roofers, fishermen, linemen, and steelworkers than there are police officers who die on the job. The difference is that people who work in those dangerous jobs usually take precautions to avoid having an accident and would never intentionally put themselves in harm's way. Further, there seldom are people who wish to cause them harm. Their peril is from the circumstances of the job, not from people who regard them with unreasoning hatred. The average steelworker may be comfortable walking a high beam but would probably not be up for tiptoeing down an alley looking for a suspect in a "man with a gun" call. Of course, I wouldn't care to walk on a high beam either.

I'm a senior citizen now, too old for anything but memories of the job that filled so much of my adult life. The profession has moved on, too. Many of the young cops don't seem to give quite as much of themselves as we did, probably demonstrating a better sense of priority than my generation had. There's more of a siege mentality, understandable with the amount of vitriol that these youngsters must feel coming their way. Any time an individual officer does something he shouldn't, they cringe, knowing that they'll come in for a share of the public outrage that will follow. In my era, we were heroes most of the time and only villains when we really deserved to be.

I'm glad that there are still people who are courageous enough to do what we did: set aside personal fear, ride a wave of adrenaline into dangerous confrontation, and rescue those who need rescuing.

25

DEATH

W hen I was about eight or nine years old, my friends and I were playing in the hills near our neighborhood when we noticed my dog sniffing at a paper grocery bag lying near some bushes. Looking into the bag, we were horrified to see what had been a new born human baby, now dead and discarded. We ran to a neighbor, who called the police, and a few minutes later led two officers to the little body. That was my first glimpse into the police world in which death is not commonplace but is commonly encountered in various manifestations.

People who die predictably, as in the case of illness or old age, are normally taken care of by other professions. Sudden unexpected death usually falls into the law enforcement venue. Other than the abandoned baby, during my first twenty-two years I had only seen a few dead people, all of them elderly and in caskets. Between the time I put on a police uniform for the first time and the day I retired, thirty-seven years later, I saw so much death, so many abruptly interrupted lives, that I can't remember them all.

One that I do remember clearly was the first fatal car accident I went to. The call was given out as a 10-52—an accident with injuries. When I arrived, several people were kneeling by a woman lying in the road. She appeared to have a broken leg but showed no life-threatening injuries, so I left her momentarily in the care of the people who were with her and went to check on the other driver. There was a car, heavily damaged on the front left corner, sitting crazily up on the sidewalk. As I rounded the vehicle, I saw the feet and lower legs of someone who appeared to be pinned under the front suspension. By that time, there were many spectators so I quickly called a group of about ten men to help me lift the car up on its side. As we did so, there was a collective gasp from the bystanders as they saw a young woman with the top of her skull sheared away. She was still alive! I carefully pulled the girl from under the car and began the hopeless task of bandaging her exposed brain. She was alive and squirming when we put her into the ambulance. She died on the way to the hospital as I knew she would.

The follow-up accident investigation revealed a stark example of how unfair life can be. The girl who died, a seventeen-year-old from the neighborhood, was stopped at the stop sign, sipping a coke, waiting for the traffic to clear. The woman with the broken leg was driving under the influence of alcohol. She was on the through street and, as she neared the intersection where the young girl waited, the drunk drifted over and collided with the left front corner of the girl's car. The young victim was not wearing a seat belt. Her car spun around from the tremendous impact, she was thrown out through the door as it opened, and the front suspension of the car came down on her head.

I had nightmares that night. My wife told me I sat up in bed and talked incoherently about "the body." Even now when I think about that accident, it all plays back like a video in my mind. For years the smell of an overheated car radiator would immediately transport me back to that scene.

For a patrol officer, dealing with dead or dying people is a daily possibility. Motor vehicle accidents happen literally every shift. Many are minor with no injuries. Some are bloody, but not as serious as they first appear. Some are so grisly that even hardened veterans feel jolted by their first look at the carnage. One night I went to a one-car accident on the freeway in which a Volkswagen Beetle had driven into the median, gone airborne, flipped into a nose down position, and hit a concrete bridge abutment top-first. The car was so flattened that it now stood about four feet tall. There was no way to tell how many people were in it. The only sign of any human presence was a woman's hand and wrist protruding through and pinned between what had been the driver's door and the door post. It was not until we were able to get help cutting away the mangled metal that we could determine that the car's sole occupant, a thirty-something woman, had died a quick, but very gruesome death. When I was done dealing with the situation at the scene, I was given an additional assignment: to go and tell the woman's husband that she had just been killed.

I don't believe there were any murders in Bloomington while I worked there. They don't happen nearly as often in the suburban communities as they do in Minneapolis or St. Paul. I did respond to several gunshot deaths but they were all suicides. Other than a situation when someone is suffering from a terminal illness, I've always felt that suicide is a permanent solution to a temporary problem. Things get better, disappointment fades, new possibilities come along. Time may not heal all wounds, but it takes the sting out of most of them. Suicide is a terrible thing to do to a family. The worst of these calls was one in which a mother had shot herself in the head with a shotgun while her three young children were watching TV in the next room. The oldest child, a girl of about eleven, had to make the emergency call with her mother's body lying a few feet away in a room with blood and brain tissue sprayed all over the walls and ceiling. I had no doubt that the shock of an unexpected shotgun blast followed by the sight of the awful aftermath of what their mother had done would put a permanent stamp on the psyche of each of those kids.

We often answered medical emergency calls. In the case of broken limbs, cuts, bruises, or other injuries, we could always be of practical assistance. When a heart stops beating or a victim quits breathing, there's a window of a few minutes for bystanders to call for emergency help and for first responders to get there. On many of these calls the window had already closed before we arrived. On those occasions, we did what we could to revive the victim but, ultimately, had to admit that he was beyond help. Our focus then shifted to helping family, friends, and bystanders deal with the reality that someone with whom they'd just been interacting was now lying dead in the next room.

From the time I went to work for the BCA in the 1970s until the mid-1980s, I didn't have to deal with death. During that time my assignments were to the Narcotics and Organized Crime sections where my main concern was keeping myself and my fellow agents alive. In 1986, I became a homicide investigator and soon began to feel the weight of this new responsibility.

The first murder I worked as "Case Agent," our term for the one in charge of the investigation, was that of a seventeen-year-old girl who had made the mistake of opening the door for the wrong man. He entered her apartment and did just about everything that a man can do to a woman—sexually brutalizing her, beating her until her face was unrecognizable, stabbing her thirty-two times, and cutting her throat until her head was nearly severed. As I bent and looked into the victim's battered face I thought, *There's only one thing I can do for this poor kid: Get the guy who did this.* After five days, working almost around the clock, we did.

In the fall of 1986, my career took a dramatic step forward when I was promoted to Special Agent in Charge of the BCA's

Bemidji Regional Office. I supervised about twenty agents, covering the north half of Minnesota, working primarily death investigations and major narcotics cases. During the next seventeen years, ending with my retirement in 2003, my group worked about 450 death investigations. I participated in many of those cases and knew the details of all of them. I visited crime scenes, examined savaged bodies, and tried to absorb all of the details that would help to tell the story surrounding the ending of a life. I assisted at autopsies, trying to take in every detail of violence done to one who, until recently, had been a living human being and now was a lab specimen. I investigated countless shootings, stabbings, beatings, and saw some murders that had been committed with unconventional weapons: a girl beaten to death with a can of vegetables, a woman strangled with a boot lace, a man bludgeoned with a "fish whacker." I sat at kitchen tables or in living rooms, talking with people who had just lost someone they cared about, trying to answer questions without telling them things they should never have to hear. I endured smells that stayed with me long after I had left their points of origin. Somewhere I have a photo that one of our crime scene techs shot as four of us were pulling a freshly-unearthed corpse from a shallow grave in the woods. The victim had been hacked to death with a machete and had been in the ground for several weeks when we found him. The picture shows four investigators with wide grins on their faces, seemingly enjoying their grisly work far too much. What was really happening, of course, was that we were all breathing through our mouths, trying to avoid the knee-buckling odor that was wafting up from the dead man.

Other than those who committed suicide, I don't believe any of the victims in our cases had an inkling before their final events began to play out that they wouldn't see another day. Some of them died because of small decisions, by them or by others, which made all the difference. One was a woman who decided to go for a walk on a rural road near her house. She invited her husband to go with her, but he was reading a book that he didn't want to put down, so he declined—he'd go with her next time. As the woman walked, she would have seen that she was approaching a beat-up car that had run partially off the road and four very rough-looking men, trying to fix a bent wheel on the car. She must have had at least some misgivings as she neared the car, but she kept walking, staying as far to the other side of the road as she could. As she rounded a curve, one of the men began to follow her, catching up with her on a remote stretch. He dragged her into a swamp where he raped her, then murdered her by stomping on her neck until her throat was crushed. He took her wedding ring and returned to his friends. If only her husband had gone with her. If only she had turned back.

Another such case involved a girl who worked in a convenience store. She was scheduled to be off but had agreed to work an evening shift for a friend. On that night, when she wasn't supposed to be there, the girl was abducted forcibly from the store, raped and murdered by a man with a long history of sexual predation. In the homicide investigators' lexicon, that was listed as a "crime of opportunity." If the predator hadn't chosen that night to stop there, if it had not been a slow night with no other customers around, if the girl hadn't worked that shift, she would have gone on with her life.

One of the most random murders I worked was that of an Anoka County jail employee who was driving to his job one pre-dawn morning. The victim was in his personal car on Highway 10, a divided highway, while a co-worker dozed in the right passenger's seat. Both were wearing police-type uniforms with Anoka County Sheriff's Department shoulder patches. According to the first account we received, the passenger woke to an explosion complete with flying glass as their car careened into the ditch. When he was able to get his wits about him, he discovered that his friend, the driver, was dead. The driver's side window had been blown out.

As we responded to that call, we were notified that a second death had occurred about thirty miles away. A man had apparently committed suicide by shooting himself in the head with a 30-caliber rifle. The shooting took place on a bridge over Highway 94, a busy interstate freeway. Subsequent investigation established that the jailer who had been murdered on Highway 10 had been shot with the same rifle used in the suicide. The man who shot himself was now our main suspect in the homicide. A few hours later, another investigator and I found ourselves in the odd circumstance of examining two bodies on gurneys positioned a few feet apart at the Ramsey County Medical Examiner's Office: the victim from the Highway 10 shooting and his apparent killer.

As we pieced things together over the next day, we came up with a scenario: The shooter, a chronic drug/alcohol user, had a violent argument with his girlfriend a short time before the Highway 10 incident. He stormed out of her house and sped away in his car in the direction of Highway 10. The timing would have been just about right for him to have reached the highway as the jailers passed the road he was on. He may well have caught a glimpse of a shoulder patch as they crossed his path. The suspect most likely then followed the jailers for several miles to the point where he rolled his passenger's window down, pulled into the left lane beside the victim's car, laid his gun barrel on the windowsill, and shot the victim, who probably never knew what happened.

Although the situation was tragic and senseless, it could have been much worse. The shooter's pockets were loaded with rifle shells and he had parked and gotten out over the freeway. It appeared to us that he may have planned to start shooting at cars as they passed below him and then just decided to turn the gun on himself.

The investigation of homicide calls for abilities that not all police officers have. One must be able to reason precisely and have the mental discipline to go no further than facts allow. Too often I saw people develop a theory and then look at the entire case through that prism. Sometimes they would "fall in love with a suspect," as we would say, and they were hardly willing to accept it when the investigation turned in another direction.

I sometimes stood at the edge of a homicide scene for twenty minutes or more, just trying to envision everything that had happened. Seeing the action in the mind's eye helped me to understand some things about the killer: Was he calm and methodical or frenzied? Did he plan to do this, or did things just spin out of control? Did he have to force an entry or was he allowed into the premises? Did it take unusual strength or skill to overcome the victim? The answers to these and many other questions are there waiting for a perceptive thinker and will help to form an image of the murderer. It also helped to understand the motive for the crime.

The other thing to be gained by imagining what took place was a fuller understanding of the kinds of evidence to be sought. Every crime scene has a finite number of pieces of evidence, not all of them easy to find or even imagine. I hated the thought of forfeiting even one of them because I wasn't smart enough to look for it.

We investigated a murder in which a twenty-year-old man was stabbed more than eighty times with a hunting knife that was left at the scene. It didn't take much thought to realize that the killer had felt some real personal animosity toward the victim. As I studied the scenario, I envisioned the mechanics of stabbing that many times and realized several things. Obviously, there would be a tremendous amount of blood spattered on the killer. He'd be literally saturated. Second, his dominant arm would have tired before he was done stabbing that many times, so he must have switched to use the other hand. Most important, though, I imagined that each time he slammed the slippery blood-covered knife into the victim, the edge of his hand would have made hard contact with the blade guard of the knife at the base of the handle. There should be significant bruising on the leading edges of both hands.

Late that evening we caught up with the killer. He had taken a shower and disposed of his bloody clothes, but he couldn't disguise the bruises on his hands that perfectly matched up with the murder weapon.

One of the things that most impressed me about the investigators I worked with was their willingness to do the job even when it cost them personally to do so. Most homicide calls came in the evening or during the early morning hours. My pager went off, usually in the middle of the night, and initiated a conversation between me and a sheriff or investigator at some freshly breaking situation. I'd get the details and tailor a response based on the circumstances. I phoned the agents who would handle the call, disrupting whatever plans they might have had for the coming day, sending them somewhere with no idea whether they'd be gone for hours or for days. If the situation warranted, I joined them.

The thing I liked least about calling the investigators at home in the middle of the night was that sometimes their wives answered the phone. To the agents, the call was a summons to their next adventure. To the wives, who all got to know my voice, it was an irritation that meant changes in plans or shifts in family responsibilities. Sometimes the muffled comments I heard in the background as a wife was handing the phone to her groggy husband were telling. What compelled these people to give up this much of their lives? They were doing something that mattered. We solved most of our homicides, although some of them took a long time to come to a conclusion. A few are still open cases. I imagine that the officers who worked these unsolved murders still occasionally wake up at night and think about them, as I do.

Frequent intimate contact with death does have an effect.

Police officers, like people in other professions who deal with the dead and dying, learn to protect themselves by remaining as emotionally distant as they can from unfolding heartbreak. Sometimes we did that pretty well, other times not. While it's true that every sudden unexpected death was a tragedy, some were more so than others. Some homicides were simply bad people doing violence to other bad people. It was a shame that it happened, but if the victim played a part in his own demise, we didn't have to work too hard to stifle our grief. Many accidental deaths or murders happened to people who were truly innocent victims. Often their last moments were so full of fear and pain and horror that even a veteran homicide investigator felt a touch of emotion as his eyes and his mind read the final paragraph of their lives. And none of us ever got used to dead children. I feel that over the years I picked up a little bit of sadness at each one of these situations. It doesn't preoccupy me, but it does visit from time to time.

26

MOST BADGES STILL SHINE

May 25, 2020, brought great trauma and grief to a family and cast a pall on the reputation of law enforcement in the United States. That was the day when George Floyd died with Officer Derek Chauvin's knee on his neck at 38th Street and Chicago Avenue South in Minneapolis. As they watched the video, played over and over on every news program, many Americans came to believe that they now knew something about the police: That cops are racist and brutal, quick to act violently; that they are constant threats, especially to young black men.

Not long after news of Floyd's death hit the media, I watched a news and commentary program on TV. A young interviewee was holding forth on the evils of American policing. "They're just waiting for a chance to use violence against innocent people," she said with fervent conviction.

My first thought was *I wonder if she's ever actually met any cops.* Whatever the answer to that question, those are broad strokes with which to paint a group of over 697,000 officers.

Here's where I believe she went off the rails. It's easy to hold generalized views of blocks of other people. It's a convenient way to organize our thoughts and to focus scorn on those who are different from us. It's also wildly inaccurate when it comes to actually understanding what individuals within the group are all about. Martin Luther King's great hope was that his children would be judged by the content of their character. That's something that can only be done individually, one human being at a time. It's too much work for someone who would rather just go with rhetoric. I have no doubt that some of those negative things are true, in greater or lesser degree, of some police officers. In the main, though, the portrayal is miles away from reality. In my years on the job, I knew and worked with hundreds of cops. Those embracing the brutal imagery will scarcely believe this: Not only did I never beat anyone; I never saw another officer do it either.

Several times I held dead children in my arms, desperately trying to breathe life back into their little bodies. I crawled in through the broken window of a mangled car to save a woman who was bleeding to death. I performed CPR, sometimes successfully, on people whose lives were hanging by a thread. I and several other officers ran into the heavy smoke of a burning building, waking people and getting them out. I rescued a woman who was being raped in a parking lot and captured the man who was attacking her. I crawled silently, inch by inch, with another officer down a darkened hallway looking for a man with a gun. I arrested murderers, armed robbers, and other violent felons, some who had guns or knives, without using deadly force. I could have, would have if they had forced me to, but didn't. I fought with people who were bigger and stronger than me, knowing that if I lost the fight I could die. I put about a mile of bandages on the wounds of accident victims. I swallowed hard and knocked on doors to tell people that a loved one had died. I attended funerals of fellow officers who had been killed while on duty. Extend these things by hundreds of thousands and you will have a picture of the lives of most cops. In a re-imagined world without police officers, I wonder who will take care of all of this.

I watched the video of the death of George Floyd. I only watched it once because that was all that I could bear. Even though some would expect me to defend or excuse what I saw there, I was simply shaken and appalled at the casual and careless end of a life.

You may have heard it said that most officers don't like misbehaving cops because they make the rest of us look bad. I'm sure that's a common feeling but it doesn't go far enough. I and many of the people I worked with have high ideals for what a police officer should be. They include such things as integrity and compassion and empathy. Those are qualities that we believe one needs to do the job as it should be done. It would be better for everyone if someone lacking in those areas found a less demanding profession.

Did former Minneapolis Officer Derek Chauvin kill George Floyd intentionally? That's too far a leap for me to make. If he did, with the always-present cell phone videos going and a score of witnesses all around, he certainly had no hope of committing the perfect crime. Astonishing arrogance, criminal carelessness, reckless contempt—I'd buy any or all of those explanations.

I'm all for accountability. If police officers break the law, overstep their bounds, or do a poor job at something, they should be held responsible for that failing. Here's the thing, though: There's no clear formula for navigating some of the violent circumstances in which they find themselves. Sometimes the assignment of the moment, articulated in realistic terms would be, "Rush to a crisis, disregard personal risk, and deal with whatever confronts you there. Save those who need saving, arrest those who need to be arrested, use force if necessary." It's a credit to all of the people I worked with that a task with that much danger and responsibility was not too much for them.

Now it seems that society has added another clause to that

assignment: "When you've done what you thought was your job, we'll review how you did. Race will be a factor in our analysis. If we disagree with your actions, we'll terrorize your family, make you sell your house to pay a defense attorney, and attempt to send you to prison." Even the sense of mission I felt in saving and protecting people wouldn't be enough to make me willing to face that threat.

These are grim times for law enforcement. I've heard complaints that it's increasingly difficult to find good people to run for political office. I'm afraid that we will soon be saying the same thing about the police profession.

Good luck to all of us.

ACKNOWLEDGMENTS

My wife, Elizabeth, is the unsung hero in all of these accounts. As a young wife with a small child, she learned to cope with ever-changing schedules and a husband who often was working when it would have been more convenient to have him at home. She frequently functioned as a single parent on holidays and special family times. As the family grew, she was the solid rock at home when I was off working long hours and loving the job too much. She let me go to work each day not knowing whether I'd come home or be a casualty in a dangerous profession. She's as true-blue as a wife could ever be and I'm so glad I found her many years ago.

My children, Jeff, Debbie, Shari, and Kerry grew up listening to many of these stories around the dinner table. When they were little, they thought everyone's dad carried a gun and worked odd hours. I was gone too much during their growing-up years, and yet they turned into fine adults.

Roger Pedersen, a Bloomington Police Officer, encouraged me to apply for a job with his department. He opened the door to what would become my life's work. I'm grateful he thought enough of me to extend that invitation. He and I remained life-long friends until his death in 2020.

Wendell Affield was a tremendous help and encouragement to me in the production of this book. He's published four books of his own. He was willing to share his knowledge of the self-publishing process and to introduce me to some very helpful people. Without his assistance I'd still be struggling to put something together.

Amanda Klejeski did the developmental edit for my manuscript. She took a pile of individual stories and made some organizational sense of them. It was only when she returned the results of her work to me that I began to believe that this could turn into a real book.

Sue Bruns did the final edit. She went through the manuscript three times, turning it into a readable finished product. She also explained to me what a split infinitive is.

Emily Enger, my formatting expert, did a fine job of turning my manuscript into a book that I'm proud to present to you, the reader.

ABOUT THE AUTHOR

Terry Smith grew up in northern Minnesota. After graduating from Grand Rapids Highschool, he attended Itasca Junior College, in Coleraine, Minnesota, and the University of Minnesota, in Minneapolis. In 1965, while finishing his university education, he worked the night shift in a gas station in Bloomington, Minnesota. In the small hours of the morning, when it had become quiet on the streets, several Bloomington Police Officers would routinely stop at the station for coffee. One night Officer Roger Pedersen gave Smith a police department application, saying, "We're hiring. Why don't you fill this out?" On such small things the entire course of one's life can change.

Smith became a Bloomington Police Officer in January, 1966, and immediately found that the job was a good fit for him. During his time at Bloomington, he worked as a uniformed officer, a crime scene technician, and an undercover narcotics agent.

In 1973 a former Bloomington Officer recruited Smith to join the Minnesota Attorney General's Organized Crime Intelligence Unit which later was absorbed by the Bureau of Criminal Apprehension (BCA). Working out of the BCA's St. Paul Office, he was an organized crime investigator, a narcotics supervisor, a SWAT team member, and a homicide investigator.

In 1986 Smith was promoted to Special Agent in Charge of the BCA's Bemidji Regional Office. He supervised all of the agency's investigations in northern Minnesota. In 2001, Smith received the Minnesota Police and Peace Officers Association honorable mention award as Minnesota Police Officer of the Year. He retired in 2003.

Smith began writing anecdotes from the world of policing for his grandchildren (leaving out the gory or tragic parts). Over time, others learned of the stories and encouraged him to publish a collection of them.

Terry Smith still lives in Minnesota with his wife, Elizabeth. For years he has taught death investigation classes for police officers and has travelled as far as Anchorage, Alaska, to teach at police seminars. He's an accomplished public speaker and enjoys telling entertaining tales about his days "on the job."

Dear Reader,

I hope you were able to get as much out of Code 4 as I intended you to.

When I wrote this book, I wanted to give you an inside look at the world of policing, both as it was in the past and it is today. I tried to be truthful and straightforward, not making myself or anyone else look better than we deserved. I hope you felt that I succeeded.

If you have the time, I'd really love a review. Reviews are a huge help to authors and I'm not exempt from that. Loved it, hated it—I'd just like to have your feedback. If you will be so kind, go to the Amazon website, find Code 4, and tell the world what you thought of it.

Thanks so much,